I08O4835

IMAGES
of America

MERCY HIGH SCHOOL OF MICHIGAN

In maroon graduation gowns, seniors from Our Lady of Mercy High School process outside its main entrance in 1956. Today's Mercy High School was called Our Lady of Mercy High School when it opened in 1945 near the intersection of Southfield Road and West Outer Drive in northwest Detroit. The Catholic all-girls high school operated at this location on the campus of Mercy College for 20 years until it relocated to Farmington Hills in 1965. The college campus remained in operation here until 2014, even after Mercy College merged with the University of Detroit to become the University of Detroit Mercy in 1990. The original building is still being used as classrooms for the Wayne County Community College District, which bought the campus from the Sisters of Mercy in 2010. (Courtesy of Mercy High School Archives.)

ON THE COVER: After a 1971 school day, these Mercy Girls await the school bus that will take them from the all-girls Catholic high school in Farmington Hills to their neighborhoods about a dozen miles away in northwest Detroit. (Courtesy of Mercy High School Archives.)

IMAGES
of America

MERCY HIGH SCHOOL OF MICHIGAN

Patricia Montemurri

ARCADIA PUBLISHING

ISBN 978-1-4671-0538-5

Published by Arcadia Publishing
Charleston, South Carolina

Printed in the United States of America

Library of Congress Control Number: 2020935154

For all general information, please contact Arcadia Publishing:
Telephone 843-853-2070
Fax 843-853-0044
E-mail sales@arcadiapublishing.com
For customer service and orders:
Toll-Free 1-888-313-2665

Visit us on the Internet at www.arcadiapublishing.com

To my favorite "Mercy Girl," Natalie Jo Montemurri Diehl,
who makes me smile and makes me proud every day

Contents

Acknowledgments

I am not a Mercy girl, but as I did the research for this book, I enjoyed the moments when I was caught in a hallway at Mercy High during class change. I would take a moment to stand still and watch the stampede of female energy course through the school. The girls' hair was often pulled up in casual ponytails or messy buns and braids. They wore ankle socks and knee socks with their skirts. Most faces didn't show signs of makeup. They talked loudly and were focused on where they were going.

Memories came flooding back. I graduated from a rival all-girls Catholic school—the long-gone Rosary High in Detroit. We didn't much care what we looked like at school, either. I have joked that in the 1970s, the big difference between going to an all-girls Catholic school and a coed one was the difference between knee socks versus nylon stockings. While nylons have fallen far out of favor as a staple of female dress, they were commonplace when I was growing up. I wore knee socks, usually fallen down around my ankles. My sister, who went to a coed Catholic school, and her other female classmates tended to wear flesh-toned nylons to impress boys.

Mercy is one of the few all-girls Catholic high schools in the Detroit area that have survived from when I was growing up. For the sake of my daughter, who is a Mercy girl, I am forever grateful for the education she received as a member of the Mercy High class of 2012.

Thank you to Mercy High president Dr. Cheryl Delaney Kreger (class of '66); Julie Earle, communications director; Jennifer Stark and Maureen Stirling ('96), codirectors of advancement; Laura Merritt Everett ('98), alumnae director; and Gina Gray ('91), of special events. Thank you to Kate Scalzi, Mercy assistant director of athletics and transportation, and Kieran Neaton ('20).

Thank you to Sr. Nancy Thompson ('50), an alumna, former principal, and archivist, and to Sr. Maureen McGarrigle ('57). Thank you to Mercy alumnae who submitted photographs for review, including Jeannette Chermside ('49), Anne Brennan MacLachlan ('49), Nancy Rouen Coles ('50), Nadine Frazier Maynard ('63), Theresa Capelli ('66), Kathleen Dul Aznavorian ('64), Brooke Potts Stambersky ('98), Annette Patrello Quillan ('66), Catherine Paler-Amaya ('85), Rochelle Chezick ('17), Patty O'Donnell ('74), and Mary Pat Hammell Conen ('76).

Thank you to Kathy Kieliszewski at the *Detroit Free Press* and my former *Free Press* colleague and friend, photographer Diane Weiss. Thank you to Hallie Smith, who supervises the spectacular *Lore* yearbook staff, and to Lynn Waldsmith, former *Detroit News* reporter turned Mercy High journalism teacher. Thank you to Robert McClain for the use of photographs from StudentandAthlete.org.

Unless otherwise noted, the photographs in this book come from the archives of Mercy High School, the Mercy High *Lore* yearbook staff, the Mercy High *Newsprint* student newspaper staff, and the Sisters of Mercy archives. Thank you also to *Oakland Press Sports* editor Jeff Kuehn and photographer Ken Swart.

This book was initially scheduled for a fall 2020 release to mark Mercy High's 75th anniversary. The team at Arcadia Publishing allowed us to postpone publication for one year because of complications caused by the COVID-19 pandemic. A special thank you goes to my Arcadia editor Caitrin Cunningham, who has been gracious and patient, and to my Arcadia proofreader, Sara Miller, kind and keen-eyed. Many thanks also go to Arcadia sales manager Mike Nieken for his assistance in publishing during a pandemic.

INTRODUCTION

Mercy High School is Michigan's largest all-girls Catholic school. It has survived to thrive through decades of upheaval and change in southeastern Michigan and draws students of all faiths and races from more than 60 communities in metropolitan Detroit.

Its opening as Our Lady of Mercy High School in northwest Detroit in 1945 forecast a boom in Catholic education in Detroit, which was the fourth-largest city in the United States at the time. In 1965, when the school moved 11 miles away to suburban Farmington Hills, Mercy was in the vanguard of the Catholic population's migration to the suburbs. When Mercy relocated, there were still 54 other Catholic high schools in the city, with 5 of them being all-girls. Today, in the city of Detroit, only 3 Catholic high schools remain open, and none of them are all-girls.

"We've been a driving force in education for more than 75 years," says Mercy president Cheryl Delaney Kreger (class of '66), EdD, who started ninth grade at the Detroit school and finished her senior year at the new school. Mercy High's foundation is rooted in the vision of the Venerable Catherine McAuley, who founded the Sisters of Mercy in Dublin, Ireland, in 1831 and once proclaimed: "No work of charity can be more productive of good to society than the careful instruction of women."

"The world needs Mercy graduates today more than ever," said Kreger. "Our alumnae are high-achieving women of faith who have found their voice, recognize social justice issues and are driven by their values. They are, as our school motto states, 'Women who make a difference.'"

Traits that have long contributed to Mercy's success prepared the school to deal with the tumultuous disruption wrought by the global COVID-19 pandemic. As Mercy prepared to graduate its hallmark 75th-anniversary class, conventional school life ceased upon government orders to shut down in mid-March 2020. Mercy High halted in-person learning for the remainder of the 2019–2020 school year. However, Mercy's early adoption of classroom technology—students have been required to use personal computer devices since 2005—made the adjustment to full-time virtual learning easier than some other schools experienced.

Mercy girls responded with innovation and resiliency. The class of 2020 senior officers helped lead the way by utilizing regular dispatches on social media to provide vital school information, advice on digital classroom learning while sequestered at home, and even cooking instructions about how to replicate the cafeteria's best-selling "Kickin' Chicken." The refrain the senior officers used to open every video broadcast was, "Wake up, Mercy. Today's a new page!" The closing send-off was, "Remember Mercy, don't count the days. Make the days count!"

When Macey Earle arrived at Mercy High as a ninth-grader, she did not know another student and was afraid she would not fit in. She found her niche in sports and student government and was a student body officer when she graduated in 2020. She helped guide other students through those first days of coping with the pandemic and disrupted traditions. The pomp of the 2020 graduation was accompanied by unprecedented circumstance. Instead of a graduation ceremony at the ornate Detroit Opera House, Mercy students were masked and socially-distanced when they received their diplomas on July 19, 2020, in the Detroit Catholic Central gym. Mercy, said Earle, always taught her to meet challenges: "It's not a place where you have to fit into a cookie-cutter stereotype of a teenage girl. You learn to embrace the authentic version of yourself."

That spirit was also at work for the 2020–2021 school year. As the pandemic raged on, Mercy reopened for in-person learning in August 2020, unlike many Detroit-area public schools. Mercy instituted a hybrid model, with half of the student body attending in person, alternating with another half who checked in virtually from home. Some Mercy students attended school online for the entire year, while most returned to a full in-person schedule in March 2021.

"Most of us walked into this year with high hopes, but also had to acknowledge that realistically, the pandemic could take away everything within a blink of an eye," wrote Delilah Coe ('21) for the *Mercy Newsprint*. "The final step is to accept that this school year is unprecedented and there is unfortunately nothing we can do to change it. Even though this is not the year we hoped for, I hope we can still make it the best."

Even with the limits imposed by the pandemic, they excelled. Mercy girls found success in the classroom, in athletics, and in maximizing life online. For example, the traditional school fall drama was replaced by an online presentation of monologues from the play *10 Ways to Survive Life in a Quarantine*. The One Love Foundation certified Mercy as a Champion School for its efforts to promote healthy relationships.

These accomplishments are emblematic of how Mercy High School seeks to educate the whole young woman academically, spiritually, socially, and emotionally. Mercy students display the diversity of metro Detroit and hail from a kaleidoscope of socioeconomic, ethnic, and faith backgrounds. While Mercy is a Catholic school, the school's students represent multiple creeds and religions. The decisions of these students (and their parents) to attend Mercy enriches the school—and reflects the real world—rather than diminishing its Catholic identity.

In the decades since the women's movement asserted itself, all-girls schools have fostered independence, self-reliance, and initiative by females. At schools like Mercy, women are always the stars, the leaders, and the top athletes—as well as the cheerleaders. Women are the class presidents, debaters, valedictorians, science-fair winners, star actresses, and those who build the stages and direct the plays—as well as the rabble-rousers.

More than 16,000 alumnae of Mercy High have led from where they are, whether that is in the workplace, as volunteers, or in their homes—and often all of these at once. They have excelled in multiple fields, including business, public service, health care, social work, entertainment, the arts, and athletics. At this time of this writing in 2021, two "Mercy Girls" were serving in high-ranking positions at Detroit-area hospitals: Margaret Dimond ('76; at McLaren Oakland in Pontiac) and Luanne Thomas Ewald ('87; as chief operating officer of C.S. Mott Children's Hospital and Von Voigtlander Women's Hospital at Michigan Medicine). Five Mercy graduates serve as elected judges in Oakland County alone. Among the school's luminaries are world-renowned golfer Meg Mallon ('81), who won 18 LPGA championships; and Diane Dietz ('77), an All-American basketball player and deputy commissioner of the Big Ten conference.

Mercy has been a leader in the use of technology since the 1960s, when a closed-circuit television studio was introduced. Such innovations have continued, with Mercy staffers providing a yearly "Tech Talk" conference for other schools. Mercy has thrice been named an Apple Distinguished School and has access to specialized training through Apple. The student tech club, named i-Wizards, runs new-student orientation for technology. The Mercy robotics team, the Riveters, have been recognized in world and state competitions. Local utility DTE Energy installed a $2.5 million, 400-kilowatt solar-panel array on Mercy's roof in 2012 to generate solar energy. Not only has Mercy been a standard-bearer in adopting technology, it has presented robust offerings in STEM field classes, digital design and learning labs, coding, and robotics. In January 2021, the College Board recognized Mercy with its Computer Science Female Diversity Award for expanding young women's access to AP Computer Science principles. Mercy's art, language, writing, and performance classes are strongly emphasized and shine in equal parts.

Sommer Woods ('95), the first Black woman to be honored with the Mercy Distinguished Alumna Award, remembers being wowed by Mercy when she visited it while at Detroit's Gesu Catholic Elementary.

"Mercy did a shadow day, and I followed a student around and I just loved it," said Woods, formerly vice president of external relations, marketing, and communications for Detroit's M-1 Rail system. Woods was raised in Detroit, and going to Mercy meant venturing out to a predominantly white school and suburb. It was the first time, she says, that she met girls with such diverse backgrounds—girls whose parents were from Asian countries such as India and China, Middle Eastern countries such as Lebanon and Egypt, or those known as Chaldeans (Catholics from Iraq).

"It was a melting pot that I enjoyed," said Woods, who runs her own firm, Woods & Watts Effect, as an inclusion, equity, and communications specialist. She credits now-retired English teacher Michael Gruber for fostering frank discussions in his English classes and as a moderator of the school's Human Relations Council, where students untangle thorny issues.

"I was allowed to grow and be strong and exuberantly and unapologetically female and who I am," said Woods.

Mercy alumna director Laura Merritt Everett ('98) laughs when she explains what attracted her to Mercy as a sophomore. The public school she attended for ninth grade started at 7:20 a.m., while Mercy clocked in an hour later. Her dad, however, was more impressed when he heard Mercy's then-principal Sr. Regina Marie Doelker talk about the school's commitment to community service.

Everett sees visions of her high school days when she steps into the hall to see girls who do not wear makeup and are content to throw on a uniform skirt and white Mercy blouse. The big difference from 25 years ago is the addition of a cell phone as an unrequired part of the uniform, but these are stowed away once in class. "It is a place where you can become your own unique person," said Everett, "and ... everyone is able to be is embraced."

President Kreger has accompanied her alma mater through many changes and challenges—and there are more to come. In southeastern Michigan, demographics portend a smaller pool of high school students for the next decade. There is also the challenge of fundraising. Graduates of all-girl schools across the country typically donate less to their alma maters than men who graduate from all-boys schools. When President Kreger was a Mercy freshman, three-quarters of the faculty were Sisters of Mercy who wore full habits. In 2021, Kreger's 12th year as president of Mercy High, the Mercy sisters no longer actively teach in school classrooms, although three serve on the board of trustees while others participate in committees and take on special projects. Several Mercy High teachers and staffers are Mercy Associates, who undergo a course of spiritual reflection with a Sisters of Mercy mentor to commit to the congregation's values and ministries.

Mercy High School is one of 54 schools in the United States and five other countries that are governed by the Mercy Education System of the Americas. When Our Lady of Mercy opened in 1945, the school was near the demographic center of metropolitan Detroit's population. Its location, at what was then Southfield Road and W. Outer Drive in northwest Detroit, came to be nicknamed the Four Catholic Corners; some even called it Little Rome. By 1954, the intersection was home to four Catholic institutions: Mercy High (on the grounds of Mercy College), the growing parish of St. Scholastica, the Little Sisters of the Poor complex (which included a nursing home), and the coed Benedictine High School. In the mid-1950s, Detroit's post–World War II population was surging.

Mercy left Detroit because it was bursting at the seams and needed more space for the baby-boomer girls who wanted to attend the high school or sought to pledge themselves to become Sisters of Mercy. Mercy did not anticipate Detroit's swift decline and shrinking manufacturing sector amid racial tensions, which were compounded by the civil unrest of 1967.

Much as it once expanded to meet demand, the Mercy campus established in 1965 will now transform to reflect evolving community needs as the number of Sisters of Mercy declines and southeastern Michigan's population base grows older. Mercy High is separated by a pond and nature preserve from a complex built by the Sisters of Mercy in 1965 to house and educate members. In 2021, the Sisters of Mercy sold the 30-acre campus to a developer of senior-living communities. Plans call for more than 250 independent and assisted-living apartments on the property. The chapel, with its triangular blue roof visible from 11 Mile Road, is one of the few buildings that will remain for reuse. The City of Farmington Hills will continue to operate the Costick Center recreation building on the site. Nearly 35 acres will be deeded to the high school and preserved as a nature conservancy, and the familiar labyrinth and an outdoor Stations of the Cross will remain for student use.

The Sisters of Mercy legacy will always have a home and live on in Mercy High, even as their Detroit-area residence is razed. Tangible reminders of their history endure. At Mercy High, stained-glass windows from the school's original location illuminate the new gathering space called

Catherine's Tea Parlor, a name that harkens to traditions dear to the Sisters of Mercy in Ireland. Adorning the school walls are crosses fashioned by Sr. Marie Henderson ('67) from concrete steps at the Detroit campus. Now, at Mercy High's main entrance, all who enter are greeted by a statue of the Blessed Mother Mary that stood at the Sisters of Mercy complex next door.

"Mercy High School will continue to be animated by the critical concerns of the Mercy Sisters and their charism," said President Kreger. "We will always graduate young women of faith who make a difference in the world and live Mercy values."

Mercy High also continues to evolve in what it offers to students. The school is exploring a program to provide students with work internships. Mercy High never had lockers lining its hallways; they were put in the basement, but students usually lugged around their books and outerwear rather than go downstairs. In 2020, the basement was converted to the M-Zone, an athletic training facility.

In June 2020, Mercy High also confronted a revolutionary discussion about racism. It was spurred by the galvanizing movement ignited worldwide after the murder of George Floyd, a Black man, by a Minneapolis police officer while in police custody. In a dialogue that largely played out across social media, some Mercy alumnae and former students described how Black students had encountered instances of racist comments and insensitivity during their time at Mercy and also brought up the need for more minorities to be represented in the school's faculty, staff, and administration. In response, Mercy organized an online forum that drew 530 students, alumnae, parents, and Mercy staff to discuss the anger and hurt and the need for change. The forum was moderated by alumnae director Everett and Distinguished Alumna Award recipient Woods.

The forum discussion was a breakthrough. Participant Megan Driver ('20) says she felt welcome from her first day at Mercy, where she joined the Inspirations Choir, the Human Relations Council, and BASE (the Black Awareness Society for Education). But she recalls instances of hearing insensitive racial comments and slurs—and she says reports about them were not adequately addressed.

"These situations have helped me become more mature, and you have to push yourself and pray for better outcomes," said Driver. She welcomes the changes underway to help Mercy's students of color know "they are beautiful and unapologetic and they can talk about what happens with support from Mercy alums and the Mercy administration."

Mercy High acknowledged the pain and anger. The school committed itself anew to fulfill a critical concern long articulated by the Sisters of Mercy, to "dismantle racism in order to become an anti-racist multi-cultural community." Mercy High instituted measures to broaden representation. Mercy hired Traci Smith to be the school's first Director of Diversity, Equity and Inclusion. The Board of Trustees Racial Task Force was formed and cochaired by Karla Rose Middlebrooks ('76), a retired senior vice president of operations finance for automaker Chrysler; and Susan Hiser, a lawyer specializing in employment issues and the mother of two alumnae. Mercy CORE (Council on Racial Equity) was established with alumnae, parents, and Mercy representatives to "engage the entire community in addressing any lingering remnants of racial inequity in thoughts, words, or deeds at our school" and to "oversee and ensure success of this visionary and far-reaching endeavor towards a Just Mercy."

In speaking to "Mercy girls" across generations and varying backgrounds, one consistent theme emerges: Gratitude for a stellar education and an environment to find one's calling and voice.

"I entered Mercy as an uncertain freshman, knowing just a few girls from public school. It didn't take me too long to find my tribe of people, both in new friends who became lifelong friends, and in new teachers who had a profound lasting effect on me," recounts Kari Zimmerer Wilson ('91), who has worked as a copy editor, social worker, and proofreader. "At Mercy, surrounded by caring teachers and lots of smart girls, I found that it was OK to be openly intelligent and ask questions. I developed my passion for writing and learning. Mercy gave me an unrivaled education, for sure, but its other gifts were even more priceless: a love of learning, a passion for social justice, an intellectual curiosity, and above all, enduring friendships."

One

Our Lady of Mercy's Detroit Heart

Students gather on the steps to the main entrance of Our Lady of Mercy High School, which opened on September 6, 1945, near the intersection of Southfield Road and West Outer Drive in northwest Detroit. It was among more than 40 Catholic high schools within Detroit, which was then the nation's fourth-largest city. "Three hundred girls entered its door," the yearbook noted, "and there was life at OLM [Our Lady of Mercy]."

These two views of the Our Lady of Mercy campus illustrate the school's location in a northwest Detroit neighborhood of working-class bungalows. The school fronted Southfield Road, a north–south artery that was expanded into a freeway during the 1960s. The intersection of Southfield Road and W. Outer Drive came to be known as the "Four Catholic Corners" and even "Little Rome" because of the other Catholic institutions at the intersection—St. Scholastic Catholic Church and School, the Little Sisters of the Poor orphanage and retirement home, and the coed Benedictine High School, which opened in 1958. Our Lady of Mercy was built for 500 students.

Our Lady of Mercy High School, in sharing a campus with Mercy College, boasted distinctive and attractive landscaping. The campus included a pond, which froze over easily for winter sports. The leafy grotto (above) was a campus landmark framed by bountiful weeping willow trees. The grotto encircled a statue of Mary, the mother of Jesus. During high school graduation, Mercy girls each took one red rose from their bouquets to place in a vase at the statue of Mary. Below is the wooden walkway that symbolically linked the high school to Mercy College.

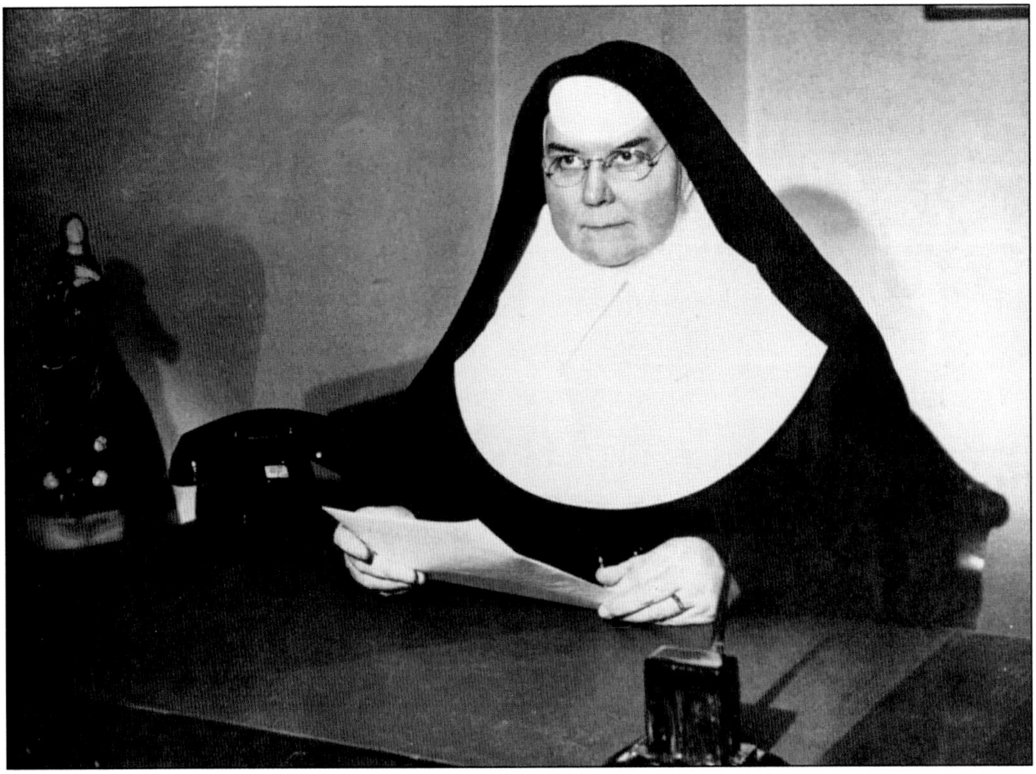

Sr. Mary Raymond (pictured) was the mother provincial, overseeing the Detroit Sisters of Mercy as they established Our Lady of Mercy High School. In 1946, in the first Our Lady of Mercy High yearbook, she wrote, "You are in a special way, children of Mary. May her example give purpose and reason to your lives and inspiration for right-thinking, acting and living. Your school is a monument to one whose life was eminently Mary-like, Catherine McAuley, Foundress of the Sisters of Mercy. From her comes the spirit and traditions which are founded on a deep, whole-hearted devotion to Mary, the model of true womanhood. I pray that you, the girls of Our Lady of Mercy School, will ever be faithful to her, your model. Then you will be true builders of a better world." The school's first principal was Sr. Mary Callista, who was assisted by 13 other Sisters of Mercy and the school's first chaplain, Rev. Robert Burroughs. The school's song was entitled "For Christ Our King, Through Mary," with words and music by Sr. Mary Vincent Meyer; one verse of the song states: "Our Lady of Mercy, we pledge to thee. Our standards of womanhood ever will be, our gift to all humanity." Jeannette Kelly Chermside ('49) was a freshman that first year. To school, she wore a maroon jumper with a Mercy crest on the left side and a beige blouse with a Peter Pan collar. She remembers the whole school voted on what to wear for graduation ceremonies. Their choice: white ball gowns set off by a bouquet of red roses in each graduate's arms. That tradition endures to this day.

Ice-skating was a popular winter pastime for students. This photograph was featured in Our Lady of Mercy's first yearbook, the 1946 *Lore*. Behind the skaters is the Mercy grotto dedicated to the Blessed Virgin Mary.

En garde for Mercy! Donatha Kubasiewicz (left) spars with Mary Moran in a duel captured for the 1946 yearbook.

These Mercy students aimed for success as they practiced archery in the late 1940s. The girls "gave it a try for the eye," noted the yearbook. In recent years, Mercy High students have established an archery team. Anyone who applies is accepted and can learn the sport and compete in tournaments.

Mercy girls often ventured out to the well-known Ray's Ranch in the once-rural suburb of Farmington to ride horses. They were often led on a "merry chase" by the school's physical education teacher, Shirley Fuhrmann, according to the 1947 yearbook. The school has maintained an equestrian team for decades.

Home economics was a required class and a staple of the curriculum. It was important for young women to learn how to sew, and home economics teacher Sr. Mary Evangeline supervised the stitching, as shown above. There also was a Future Homemakers of America club. In the Mercy classroom kitchen (below), the students were instructed on the proper icing of gingerbread cookies.

Girls' half-court basketball was an intramural sport. The 1947 Our Lady of Mercy intramural champs were from Room 204. The intramural volleyball champs were from homeroom 110, according to the 1947 yearbook.

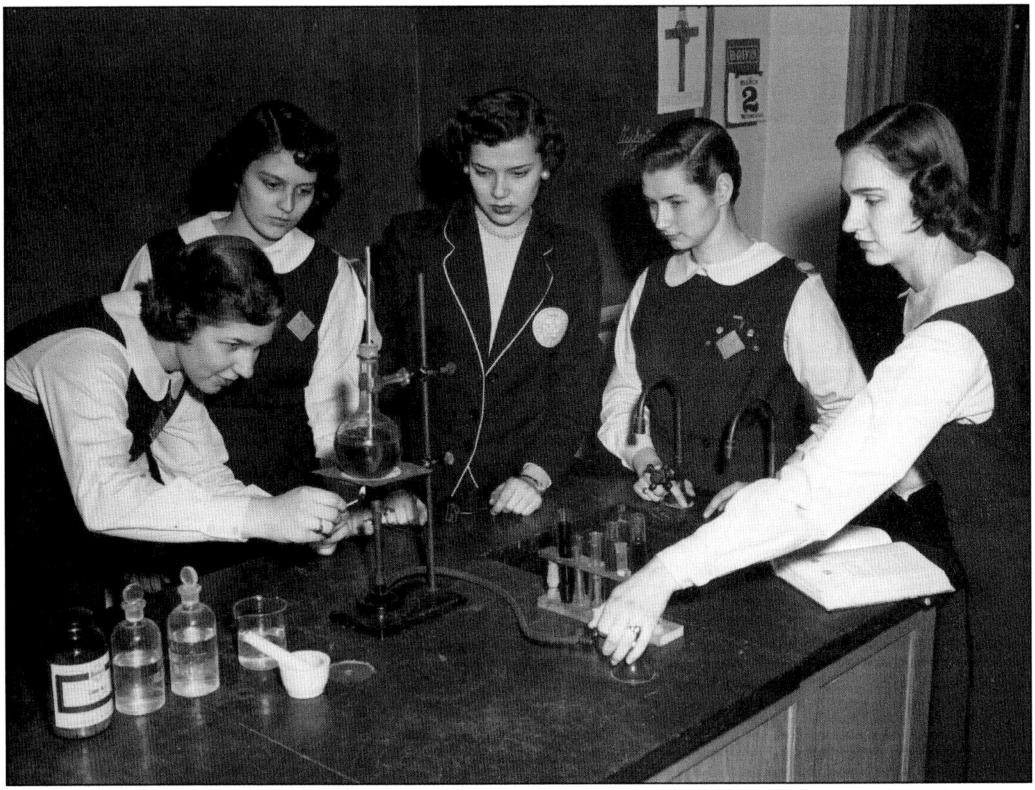

Chemistry class demands concentration. The student on the far right is Monica Kostielny, who graduated in 1954 and joined the Sisters of Mercy. She returned to the school and worked in the advancement office.

It is traditional for Catholics to honor Mary, the mother of Jesus, during the month of May. One of the many titles bestowed by the church on the Blessed Mother is Mary, Queen of May. Catholic schools hold a service known as the May Crowning, and it was a coveted honor to be chosen to place a crown on a statue of Mary, typically in an outdoor setting. In this image, the 1949 May Crowning is taking place outside.

Each October brought another event to honor Mary, the mother of Jesus. The Marian Procession was held in October and united students from Our Lady of Mercy High School and Mercy College and staff from Mt. Carmel Mercy Hospital. The hospital was located at W. Outer Drive and Schaefer Avenue, about two miles east of the Mercy campus. One goal of the Marian Procession was to encourage Catholics to recite the Rosary. In 1950, when this photograph was taken, Detroit was at its peak population of 1.8 million, boosted by European immigrants and Black migrants from Southern states who settled in the area for jobs. At that time, the city's population was about

65 percent Catholic. The intersection of Southfield Road and W. Outer Drive was nicknamed the Four Catholic Corners because the intersection's landscape was defined by four Catholic institutions. Just east of Mercy College, on the intersection's northeast corner, the Little Sisters of the Poor had built a facility in 1928 for the aged and poor. It operated for several decades until it was replaced with a shopping center. The building in the background of this photograph was the main classroom building for Mercy College, which was all-girls when it was founded in 1941. The building fronted W. Outer Drive.

Mercy's tradition of producing quality musicals and dramatic plays goes back to its earliest years. In 1949, the school staged the musical *On Top of Old Smokey.* It was common for girls to play the men's roles in productions until the mid-1960s.

Rev. Robert Burroughs was OLM's chaplain and theology teacher for nearly two decades after the school opened. In the 1947 yearbook, he wrote of the "five traits of virtue" that a Mercy girl should embody: "A sense of gravity of things worthwhile; second a generosity of soul to help you be considerate of God and others; thirdly a sincerity that will influence others rather that they be led astray; fourthly, earnestness in the expression of faith, hope and love; and lastly a kindness in looks, words and deeds that will be a fountain of gladness to freshen . . . all you contact."

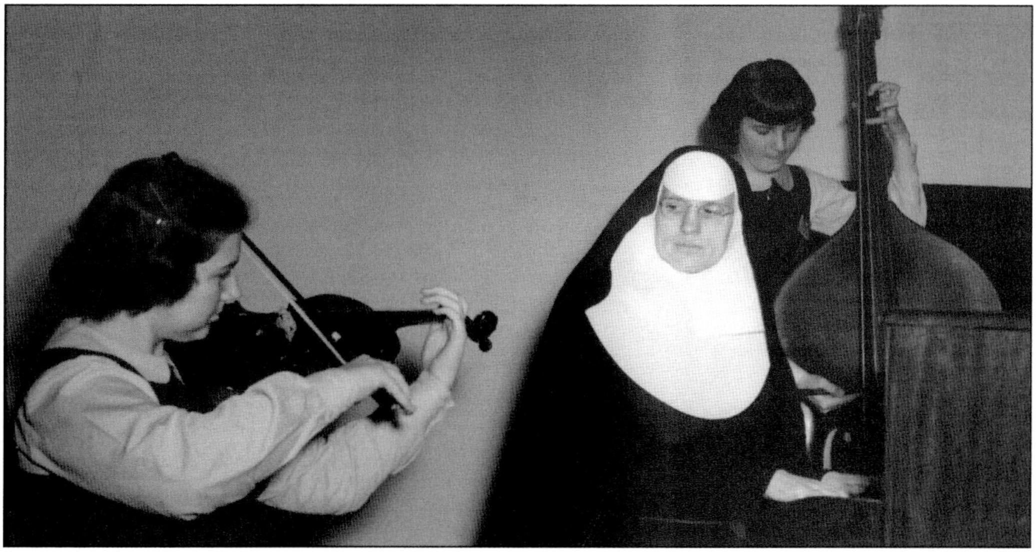

Music instruction was a vital component of the school's curriculum. Girls performed instruments ranging from strings to keyboards to drums in its orchestra. Above, Sr. Mary Albertine guides a student through violin practice. In the below photograph, which is from the mid-1950s, orchestra instructor Daniel Ryan conducts the OLM Orchestra.

The OLM Sodality League did its part to fight the Cold War, mobilizing to end the Soviet Union's spread of communism during the 1950–1951 school year. The poster on the back wall depicts communism as a serpent to be vanquished by praying the Rosary. The students around the table are, from left to right, (seated) Patricia Gillette, Gail Bowler, Marilyn Rohr, Mary K. Whiting, Mary Martha McKeown, Judith McCartney, and Romayne Carletti; (standing) Mary Joyce Geraci, Agnes Schettenhelm, Patricia Brick, Margaret McKenna, Margaret Denomme, and Elizabeth Quigley.

The teaching of shorthand was a staple of high school curriculums in the 1950s. Shorthand was viewed as a vital skill for young women seeking to work as secretaries and in other office jobs after graduating from high school. Long before the widespread use of tape recorders or mobile phones, shorthand allowed a practitioner to take dictation using symbolic writing.

There were several formal dances throughout the school year. Above, young people are waltzing the night away on the dance floor at Lovett Hall in Dearborn's Greenfield Village at a 1950s-era Our Lady of Mercy prom. In the photograph at right, a Mercy girl introduces her date to Sr. Mary Victorine near the statue of the Blessed Mother Mary during a dance at the high school.

Mercy faculty are pictured having a picnic by the pond in August 1952. From left to right, going clockwise around the table, are Srs. Mary Laurentina, Mary Leocadia, Mary Carmen, Mary Albertina, Mary Doris, Mary Isadore, Mary Florentine (partially hidden), Mary Edna Marie, Mary Imelda, Mary Claudia, Mary Victorine, Mary Ignatius, and Mary Michael.

At the start of a school year around 1955, Mercy faculty marked the day by posing for a photograph. From left to right are (first row) Srs. Mary Albertine Baumann and Mary Cojetea (Barbara) Gallant; (second row) Srs. Mary Ignatius Denay, Mary Victorine Rapin, Mary Jeanne Salois, and Mary Florentine; (third row) Srs. Mary Leocadia Starr, Mary Carmen Brown, Mary Laurentina Taffee, and Mary Protase.

After OLM opened, it was not unusual for a Mercy girl to contemplate becoming a Sister of Mercy. Many graduates recount how Mercy sisters inspired them. At right, Srs. Mary Ignatius Denay (left), Mary Protase (center) and Mary Jeannette Schneider operate an information booth at the school around 1952. The unidentified woman in the white veil is a novice who was in her second or third year of religious life. The unidentified woman at far right is a postulant in her first year of convent life and is contemplating whether this is a calling she wants to pursue. Below, these women were all graduates of Our Lady of Mercy High and were pursuing their vocations in 1953.

Cleo Shellenberger (seated, center) was one of the school's original lay faculty members. She retired from teaching Latin in 1952. She is pictured here with other staff members; they are, from left to right, Eileen Wagner, Jeannette Falmer, Ruth Summerill, an unidentified woman, Luella Starr, and Frances Rasch.

Our Lady of Mercy prepared women to enter college after graduation but also to enter the workforce of the 1950s. For women who did not go to college or get married and start families, the telephone company offered opportunities for young women who wanted to work as switchboard operators. Michigan Bell Telephone Company advertised in the 1956 *Lore* yearbook.

In this photograph, Mercy students consider their choices from a selection of albums featuring classical music. Outside class, however, students were tuning into the beginnings of rock and roll.

Mercy seniors toiled to publish the school newspaper, *Newsprint*. In this photograph from March 18, 1958, Mercy girls study the latest edition of the *Detroit News*. The headline story recounted how the night before, television viewers had witnessed a live broadcast of a two-hour surgery to improve blood flow to a man's leg at Henry Ford Hospital in Detroit. Pictured are, from left to right, (seated) Nancy Stenger and Joan Dulas; (standing) Paula Schimmel, Rosemary Dick, Diane Linhard, and Rosalie Rebain.

During Lent, Mercy girls often volunteered to dedicate themselves to saying the Rosary each day. "Through Mary is the surest way to the Kingdom," noted a yearbook. "The daily Rosary is our tryst with our Mother Beloved."

These students are preparing for the school's candlelight ceremony, when Mercy students would form a ring around Mercy Lake, as they called the pond outside the school doors. Seniors received their class rings on the night of the ceremony. The candlelight symbolized faith shining through the fog of life. "We have no fear, no dread, that our light shall go out, or that we shall lose the way! For our hands rest firmly in the hand of Mother Church. And God's love guards our candles and God's Mother, our hearts," noted a yearbook about the onetime tradition.

Every student was required to take a music class, and musical chorale was the top choice. This is one such chorale from the late 1950s. In yearbook photographs, the students who participated in chorale were listed according to their vocal ranges—soprano, second soprano, or alto.

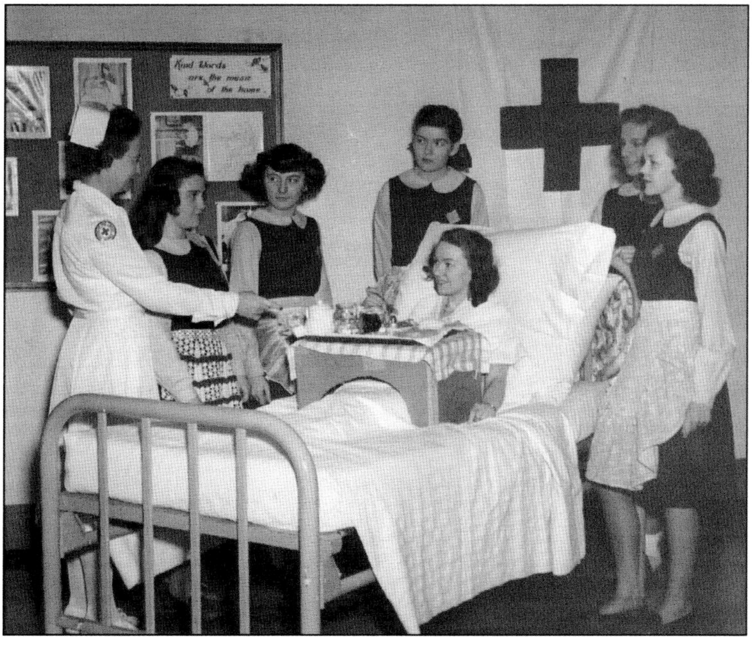

Members of the Future Nurses Club posed for a photograph with a real nurse and a fake patient at the school. Nursing was one of the top majors pursued by students who entered Mercy College, located next to Our Lady of Mercy, which provided many staffers for the nearby Mt. Carmel Mercy Hospital run by the Sisters of Mercy.

The Arc de Triomphe Club was formed by students who pursued French language studies and was named after the Paris monument that honors the soldiers of the French Revolutionary and Napoleonic Wars. The club's 1956–1957 officers are pictured during a club-sponsored dance. French was the most popular foreign language taught in the United States during the 1950s, but by the next decade, it had been supplanted by Spanish, which remains the most popular today.

Mercy girls took home top prizes in local, statewide, and Catholic school competitions that featured public speaking and dramatic interpretation. They competed in categories such as Humorous Reading, Interpretative Reading, Discussion, Dramatic Monologue, Dramatic Dialogue, Narrative Reading, Lyric Poetry Reading, and Radio News Commentary.

The poster over this congregation of Mercy girls in the 1950s reads: "Sweet Jesus, Teach Us the Way to Thy Love."

This image shows an early version of an enduring Mercy tradition—the "Moving Up" ceremony at the end of the school year. It started in the 1950s and involves a tradition in which the freshman class sits in the back of the auditorium, while seniors sit up front. In a ceremony held on the last day of classes, the seniors process out of the auditorium in their caps and gowns, while the other classes snake through row after row of seats to their new positions for the coming school year.

Our Lady of Mercy graduation ceremonies were marked by tradition. The school banner and the US flag were carried by the rising senior class officers, who led graduates out of the school's McAuley Auditorium, named after the Venerable Catherine McAuley, the Irish foundress of the Religious Sisters of Mercy. This tradition continues today.

Here, Our Lady of Mercy class of 1957 graduates, wearing white gowns and carrying bouquets of roses, are surrounded by family and friends as they make their way into the school auditorium. Behind them is the main building of Mercy College.

It was a memorable moment when OLM graduates gracefully cascaded down the auditorium steps following graduation. Red roses offered a striking contrast to the white gowns worn by the class of 1956.

The Our Lady of Mercy pond was the backdrop for this meeting of the 1956–1957 ninth-grade officers. Pictured here are (left to right) Rose Marie Bruno, Marcia Jo Pais, Linda Werthmann, and Mary Ellen Howard—all 1960 graduates. Howard, as a Mercy sister, became a nurse and hospital administrator. She was the CEO of Mercy Hospitals in Grayling and Muskegon before returning to Detroit to establish the Cabrini Clinic, which offers health care to the needy. Werthmann also became a Sister of Mercy and a social worker.

Pictured at a swim meet in the 1958–1959 school year against archrival Immaculata High School, Aggie McDonell dives for the Mercy Marlins. "Beauty and gracefulness of motion" are part of her style, noted the 1959 yearbook. The swim team's mascot was a stuffed-animal toy named Woofie.

These members of the 1963 freshman chorale, shown wearing new beige, blue, and maroon plaid skirts, were in a school bursting with more than 600 students. By the time of their junior year, these Mercy girls were at a new campus in Farmington Hills. "As school days stampede to their end in the ocean of summer vacation, Mercy's anticipation increases at the thought of relocation in a luxurious new building," noted the 1965 yearbook. "Mercy will once again stand new and proud, awaiting the students who will write her success story of the next 20 years."

Two

Mercy Moves to the Future

In 1965, Our Lady of Mercy erected a state-of-the-art school with the capacity for 1,200 students on former farmland—with a barn silo still nearby. The original school, located in Detroit, had been built to accommodate 500 to 600 girls. Before the start of the 1965–1966 school year, Mercy was relocated to the corner of 11 Mile Road and Middlebelt Road in Farmington Hills, about 11 miles northwest of the school's Detroit location. In the background, a new housing subdivision is under construction. There were many innovations to come in the decades ahead. The new school brought new changes; students could move freely through halls at the change of class rather than walk single file in silence, as they had for many years at the old school. And they could wear loafers instead of saddle shoes, remembers Dr. Cheryl Delaney Kreger, who was one of the students who made the transition. She came back to the school in 2010 as the president of Mercy High. She was among 206 young women who graduated from the new school in 1966.

These photographs show some of the new campus under construction. Above, a December 1964 image shows the south side of the school, along 11 Mile Road, eight months before it opened. Although the school opened in September 1965, the below image shows that in late October of that year, the parking lot still awaited paving at the school's southeast entrance, with the spire of the chapel rising above it. The architects, the Detroit firm of Giffels & Rossetti, also designed downtown Detroit's convention center, Cobo Hall, which is now known as the TCF Center. Farmington Hills was a small Detroit suburb when Mercy relocated there. From 1960 to 1970, the area's population grew from 6,881 to 10,329, according to US Census data. In 2019, its population was estimated at about 80,000. Next door to the new Mercy High, the Sisters of Mercy erected a campus for housing and training new members of the congregation. The complex included a residence, classrooms, recreational structures, and a chapel with a soaring blue-tiled roof visible from 11 Mile Road. The chapel became the site for the weddings of many Mercy High alumnae. In 2021, as the local Sisters of Mercy aged and the congregation's numbers declined, a decision was made to sell the landmark property. The Mercy Sisters sold the property to a developer of senior-living residences. The chapel is one of the few buildings that may remain for reuse. The City of Farmington Hills will continue to operate the Costick Center recreation building on the site. Nearly 35 acres will be deeded to Mercy High as a nature conservancy.

In the above image, Sr. Mary Victorine, Our Lady of Mercy principal, greets visitors at an open house at the new school. Sr. Mary Victorine was the assistant principal at the Detroit school beginning in 1946 and became principal of OLM in 1952, serving in that role until 1969. She presided over the school's growth from about 300 students to 1,300 across both the Detroit and Farmington Hills locations. From 1972 to 1992, she was the first director of pastoral ministry at St. Joseph Mercy Hospital in Ann Arbor.

The new school has floor-to-ceiling windows that look out on multiple courtyards. These two Mercy girls are taking a study break in one of the light-filled alcoves.

Traditions born at the Detroit school were carried on at the new building. This especially applied to the graduation ceremony. In formal white gowns, each carrying a dozen red roses, members of the class of 1966 would ring the sidewalks and an outdoor courtyard for graduation day and the awarding of their diplomas. Below, a member of the junior class carries the flag, surrounded by graduating seniors.

Other big changes accompanied the move to Farmington Hills. The Mercy Sisters teaching staff, embracing the spirit of change unleashed by the Second Vatican Council, began wearing a modified habit, as seen here. The traditional habits of Catholic nuns were based on medieval-era dress. But with the Catholic Church's embrace of modern reforms, such as using native languages instead of Latin during Mass, women religious orders were given more freedom in choosing their clothing. Many congregations of Catholic nuns shortened the length of their habits and wore modified veils. In later years, many sisters wore conventional clothing instead of habits. Pictured from left to right are: (first row) Srs. Mary Imelda Boyle, Mary Leone Archambeau, Mary Dolores, Mary Victorine Rapin, and Mary Bernarda Maclean; (second row) Srs. Mary Esther Heuss, Mary Phyllis Kaminski, Mary Callista Young, Regina Marie Doelker, Mary Ignatius Denay, and Mary Peter Vaillancourt; (third row) Srs. Mary Martina Begin, Mary Ann Elizabeth Bauer, Mary Marjorie Allen, Mary Leocadia Starr, Mary Loyola Sabourin, Ellen Mary, and Mary Margaret Brown; (fourth row) Srs. Mary Berenet, Mary Gretchen Elliot, Mary Carmen Brown, and Mary Vincent Meyer. It was common for many Sisters of Mercy to have the name "Mary" as part of their full religious names; however, they were usually addressed as Sister Martina rather than Sister Mary Martina.

Mercy High has been a premier Michigan school for young artists. One of its legendary art teachers was Sr. Mary Ignatius Denay, whose students won awards in national arts competitions for 35 years in a row. Above, she is working on one of the many mosaics that continue to grace the halls today. Below, she stands in the back of a drawing class at Mercy in 1967. Born in rural Pinconning, Michigan, she entered a Sisters of Mercy convent in Grand Rapids one month before her 15th birthday. In honor of her 80th birthday, in 1987, donors contributed to an endowed scholarship in her name. Each year, a student is awarded the Sister Mary Ignatius Scholarship.

Sr. Mary Ignatius Denay is shown reviewing a piece of art crafted by a Mercy student in 1967. When she retired from the school, her students gave her a rocking chair. Even in retirement, she continued to work on mosaics and sculptures.

Sr. Mary Victorine Rapin (left) and Sr. Mary Ignatius Denay were good friends and colleagues. Sister Mary Victorine died in 2004 at age 95 after serving as a Sister of Mercy for 77 years. Endowed scholarships named after both women are given annually to students who need financial assistance.

The Mercy High Daddy-Daughter Dance is another long-running tradition. In this photograph are an unidentified father and Mercy student at the 1966 Pop's Hop, along with an image of a mouse in a top hat. There have been variations in the style of the daddy-daughter dance. During some years, square dancing was on the dance card.

Ready for a Mercy prom are, from left to right, Susan Lertola, Lori Tiseo, Theresa Capelli, and Patricia MacDermott, members of the class of 1966. The girls had gathered at Capelli's house in Detroit. (Courtesy of Theresa Capelli.)

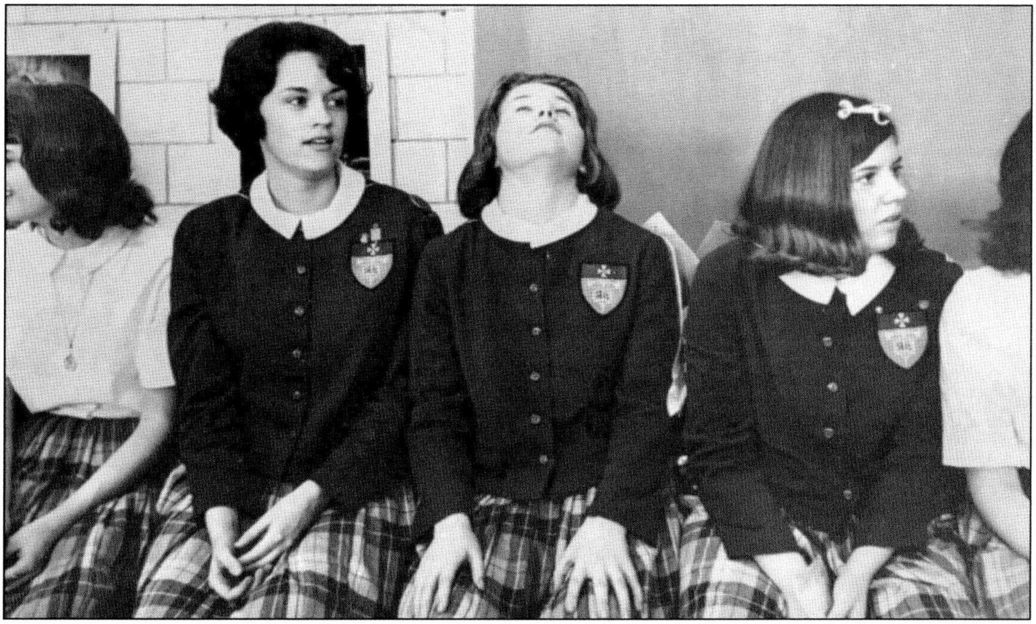

These Mercy class of 1966 girls are just hanging out. They include Ruth Butler (second from left), Barbara Rozak (center), and Sharon Torrie (second from right). They are wearing the uniform Mercy girls donned from fall 1962 until 1969.

These Mercy High editors of the yearbook, *Lore*, are leaning on each other to get the keepsake publication finished. This *Lore* team included, from left to right, Maureen Forget ('70), Diane Chermside ('70), Pam Starr ('70), Mary Salsinger ('70), and Kathy Kolbe ('69).

Mercy offered students the chance to host an in-house daily broadcast on WOLM. The class of 1972 broadcasters pictured here include, from left to right, Lisa Dailey, Denise Kelley, Maureen Bailey, Irene Schweyer, Pat Rajewski, Cecilia Bolan, Carol Skelton, and Nancy Calice.

Louise Scudlo was a legendary English teacher at Mercy from the late 1960s through the '90s. Carolyn Witte ('67), who was an English teacher and Mercy principal, recalls Miss Scudlo's impact. "She was my English teacher at Mercy and is the reason I chose that career. She was also my dearest colleague and friend when I returned to Mercy as a faculty member. She was a model for me of what a teacher at Mercy could be." Ruth Butler ('66), a *Grand Rapids Press* journalist, wrote this about Scudlo: "Her passion helped me fall in love with Salinger and made it clear that Antigone was a woman to be admired."

When a young lady attends an all-girls school, one of the skills she might acquire is learning how to ask boys out on dates. Many formal dances are part of the Mercy school year, including homecoming and A-Ball. There were boys to meet from Detroit Catholic Central, University of Detroit High School, and other all-boys schools in the area. At right, away from the dance floor, Joann Bok ('81) shares punch with Steve Moor.

It did not matter that the 1974 Detroit Tigers baseball team recorded a losing season. The team finished with a 72–90 record—19 games behind the American League East champion Baltimore Orioles. Mercy girls were serious fans, as demonstrated by the "Mercy Loves You Tigers" sign on the bus.

Boom boxes first became popular in the late 1970s. It is not known what song these Mercy girls were grooving to, but it must have had a good beat.

Sr. Camille Kelley was the principal of Mercy High from 1969 to 1978. She was also the first student to enroll when Our Lady of Mercy was founded in 1945 in Detroit. Her parents heard that the new high school was being built and told a Sister of Mercy they knew to sign up their daughter. Sister Camille, ('49), who died in April 2021, was the first Mercy High graduate to become principal of the school, but several other alumnae followed in her footsteps.

The first time these Mercy High seniors in the class of 1980 wore their maroon caps and gowns was at a Catholic Mass for the blessing of their school rings, a tradition that continues today.

Plaid uniforms returned in 1982. This Mercy student is stylishly studying in a carrel in the school library. Today, Mercy High has a media center, which has far fewer books on the shelves because of students' reliance on digital devices to access information.

Members of the 1975–1976 *Lore* yearbook staff are shown pondering an image. They are led by teacher Betty Griffiths (in the foreground). Behind her are, from left to right, unidentified, Mary Pat Lang ('77), and Mary Pat Hammell ('76). For several years in the 1950s, Mercy did not produce a yearbook. Instead, students elected to put together a literary journal. (Courtesy of Mary Pat Hammell Conen.)

To introduce newcomers to the school, Mercy High matched ninth graders with twelfth graders in the Big Sister/Little Sister tradition. In this picture from the 1982–1983 school year, (left to right) Rita Trent, Mary Duwel, Kris DeAlexandria, and Jennifer Richardson are using the hats on their heads to denote who is a Big Sister and who is a Little Sister.

The 1977 senior luncheon drew a hungry crowd. Along with the food, there were plenty of laughs, as evidenced by the grin on Marie Jelonek's face (she is standing in the center of the photograph). (Courtesy of Mary Pat Hammell Conen.)

The Mercyaires have entertained audiences since 1961. The vocal group has performed across the metro Detroit area and on its most famous stages. Currently, the group consists of rising sophomores, juniors, and seniors who audition in March. The chorale works with a choreographer during a weeklong summer camp. The Mercyaires have consistently earned top ratings at district and state solo and ensemble festival and choral festival competitions. Pictured here are the members of the 1991–1992 Mercyaires, who performed with legendary vocalist and actress Rosemary Clooney in a scholarship benefit for the school. From left to right are (first row) Julie Vaquera, Cristina Mercader, Valencia Davis, Leah Duncan, and Marjon Parham; (second row) Adrienne Hill, Barbara Sullivan, Amy Jennette, Felicia Squaire, Lizbeth Spink (behind Felicia Squaire), Jen Greening, and Erin Scheffler; (third row) Jennifer Jackson, Stephanie David, Cicely Mitchell, Mary Gormley, Catherine Worth, Bree Sutton, Abha Mangrulkar, Chandra Berger, and Poornima Paidipaty.

In March 1992, Rosemary Clooney sang with the Mercyaires in the Mercy High auditorium for a scholarship benefit. She was a graduate of Cincinnati's Mercy High School and one of the world's best-known singers during the last century. The Mercy auditorium is named after her. The Mercyaires accompanied Clooney, the Detroit Symphony Orchestra, and another renowned song-stylist of yore, Mel Torme, at the Fox Theatre, as well as at Detroit's Orchestra Hall and Meadowbrook. Rosemary Clooney died in 2002 at age 74. Actor George Clooney is her nephew.

Larry Teevens's career as a music teacher spanned from 1961 to 2001. He was adept at shaping the Mercyaires into one of the finest high school singing groups in the state. During his tenure, the Mercyaires performed as many as 60 concerts per year. Often, when the Mercyaires performed, Teevens made a point to call up any Mercyaires alumnae in the audience to join the group on stage for a rendition of "Ave Maria." A local bandleader introduced singer Rosemary Clooney to Teevens and the Mercyaires when Clooney was booked to sing at a Sterling Heights club in the 1980s. Teevens mentioned to Clooney that he had sung with her sister Betty Clooney when Betty had a show on local television station WXYZ-TV (Channel 7). After that initial meeting, the Mercyaires performed with Clooney on 10 different occasions.

Here is a sampling of Mercy High uniforms over the years, including a blue gym uniform (second from left).

Mercy girls dove deep into policy issues affecting a variety of countries as participants in the Model United Nations club, also known as Model UN or MUN. From left to right are Nancy Bokshan ('81), Phyllis Fodale ('82), and Marie Fodale ('81). Mercy competed against other schools in simulation activities and debates to learn about diplomacy and international relations in a manner similar to that used by diplomats at the actual United Nations headquarters in New York City.

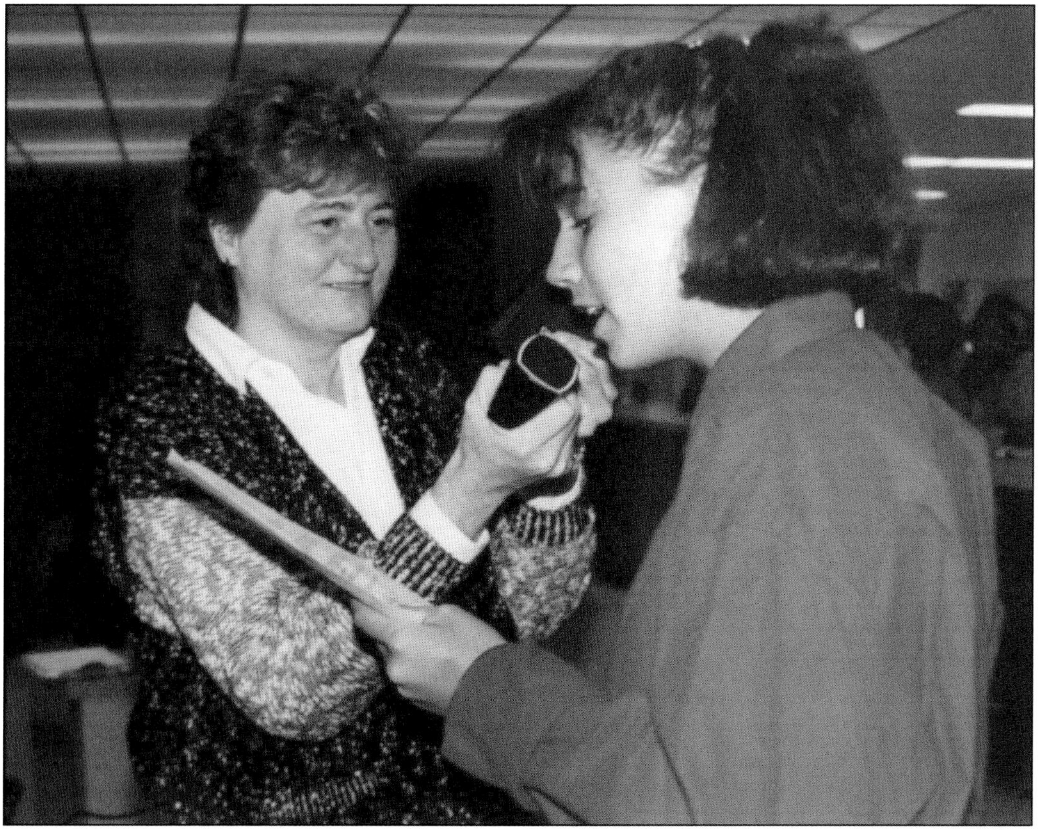

Jonell Linskey, also known as Miss Linskey, is an institution at Mercy High, where she taught religion for her first decade and then became dean of students. She retired in 2014 after 47 years at Mercy. Above, Linskey (left) and student Maura Pheney ('91) entertain the student body with their morning announcements in 1991. In recent decades, she roamed the halls on a scooter, as shown at right. At the annual Mercy High auction, one day's use of the scooter by a student was offered to the highest bidder. Mercy alumna Margaret Dimond ('76), who is now the CEO of McLaren Oakland Hospital in metro Detroit, credits Linskey's frank class discussions on death and grief as her inspiration for becoming a social worker for cancer patients and pursuing challenging graduate degrees on her course to becoming a hospital administrator. In a 2014 note to Linskey, Dimond wrote, "Simply put, you changed my life."

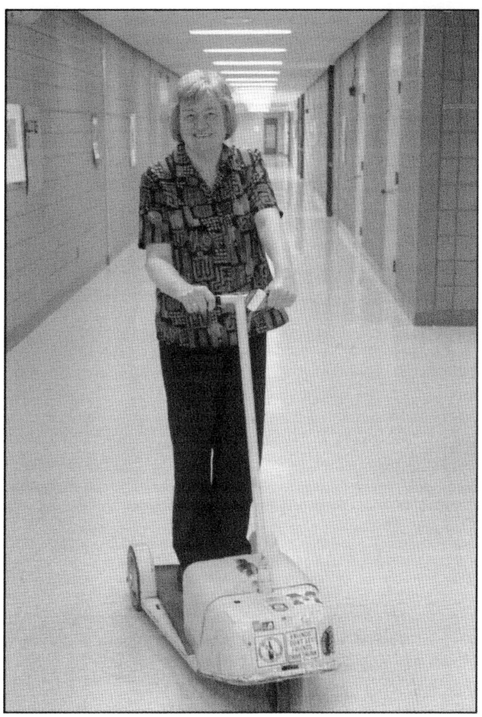

These are familiar signs around Farmington Hills, because Mercy High has won 27 state championships in sports.

During Spirit Week at Mercy, students go creatively crazy to express their loyalty to the school. Keeping it fun at the September 1997 Spirit Week are, from left to right, (first row) Brooke Potts, Jennifer Ermatinger, Theresa Franzinger, Katie Zarowitz, and Miosha Vaughn; (second row) Alexia Madias, Erin Morgan, and Erin McConnell. (Courtesy of Brooke Potts Stambersky.)

When the Detroit Red Wings won hockey's Stanley Cup in 1997, a total of 42 years had passed since the squad had last reigned as champions. So, it was a definite cause for glee when the Stanley Cup came to visit Mercy High. Above, Mercy principal Sr. Regina Marie Doelker (just left of the cart) greets Red Wings officials escorting the Stanley Cup. Below, biology teacher Gerry Meloche hoists the cup aloft.

Mercy's Human Relations Council (HRC) is a club founded in 1979 by English teacher Michael Gruber, who taught English for 40 years before his retirement in 2017. It provides an avenue for students to ask questions and discuss issues—some of them controversial—in an atmosphere of respect. HRC members from the 1980–1981 school year are pictured here. That year, the HRC sponsored a Black Awareness Week that featured gospel concerts, films on African American historical events, and a soul food lunch.

The Mercy Mothers' Club organizes multiple events to help Mercy students and staff throughout the year. Members decorate the school and chaperone activities for the all-night graduation party held inside the school, and they help cater an annual luncheon for teachers and staff. Nancy Auffenberg (farthest left), mother of Mercy alumnae Caroline and Elizabeth Auffenberg, was the president of Mercy Mothers' Club in 2005, when the club served a buffet meal to teachers.

Every May, Mercy High holds a Catholic Mass honoring the school's patroness, St. Mary, Our Lady of Mercy. As in the first years of Mercy High, there is a crowning ceremony in which a student is selected to place a floral crown atop the statue of the Blessed Mother. Shown participating in the 1999 crowning are seniors Elizabeth Mathis (left), Ami Bhatt (center), and Norell Kirma. The school also invites mothers, aunts, and special women in the students' lives to attend in recognition of Mother's Day.

In Autumn 1999, Mercy's German Honor Society celebrated Oktoberfest. Pictured here are, from left to right, (first row) Nora Clancy, Nadia Hamade, Andrea Gorecki, and Katherine Matous, with Maureen Mathews on the floor; (second row) Bahareh Aslani, Carol Flanigan, Alena Acker, teacher Frau Raya Czerkasski, Aleka Kruszewski, Courtney Skiles, and Cara Smith. Czerkasski taught German and Latin at Mercy for 33 years; she was a Holocaust survivor and an immigrant from the former Soviet Union. She told her students that her skills in foreign languages helped save her life. (Courtesy of Maureen Matthews Wentworth.)

Heidi Ewing commanded the bullhorn to start the Big Sister/ Little Sister picnic in 1989. She was voted by her classmates as the 1989 graduate most likely to be elected president of the United States, and she has made an impact with her voice and vision ever since. According to the *Detroit Free Press*, Ewing is "a leading force in documentary films." She and codirector Rachel Grady were nominated for an Academy Award in 2007 for "Best Documentary (Feature)" for *Jesus Camp*. Ewing and Grady also codirected *Detropia*, which was released in 2012 and won awards at several film festivals. In 2020, Ewing released her first fictional feature film, *I Carry You with Me*.

Art surrounds the students at Mercy High School. About half of all Mercy students take an art class each year. This mosaic was crafted by the late Sr. Mary Ignatius Denay, who is considered the founding mother of artistic expression at the school.

Three

FEAR THE FISH

No sport has won more acclaim for Mercy High athletes than swimming and diving. From the time of the Marlins' first state championship (in 1972) to its most recent (in 2019), the Marlins have collected 11 state championships. The team brought home five consecutive state titles in 2007, 2008, 2009, 2010, and 2011. Its latest championship, in 2019, was the third in a row. Nikki Barczak (above, class of '11), swam on four championship teams. She is shown here in a 2007 photograph from her freshman year. Barczak won four individual state titles and was a team captain her senior year. In 2010, she was on a 200-yard freestyle relay team that set a state record of 1:35:32; this remains the third-best time for the event. The other swimmers on that team were Taylor Steffl, Elliott Schinella, and Sato Kakihara. Also in 2010, Barczak, Olivia Samoray, Kakihara, and Maria Bargardi set a record time of 3:27.24 in the 400-yard freestyle relay. Mercy High offers 19 sports in which the school is an annual contender for Catholic League championships and in statewide competitions. The school's nickname, the Marlins, has sparked creative chants and slogans, including "Fear the Fish." (Courtesy of the *Detroit Free Press*; photograph by Patricia Beck.)

Thanks to the coaching of Deloris Yaeger, Mercy's swim team first rose to prominence in 1972. That was the inaugural year for a girls' state championship swim tournament, and the school, then known as Our Lady of Mercy, claimed it. The pool at Mercy High is named the Deloris Yaeger Natatorium in her honor, and the Catholic League's scholar-athlete award for girls also is named after her. She also coached the all-boys Detroit Catholic Central High's swim team. Here, she is pictured after receiving the Detroit-area Catholic League Person of the Year award in 1987.

Maddie Loniewski is shown on the block during a preliminary round at the 2011 Michigan state championship meet, where Mercy finished first. In 2012, Loniewski was a state champion in the 200-yard individual medley. She and teammates Roxanne Griffore, Alaina Skellett, and Kathleen McGee were first-place finishers in the 200-yard freestyle relay at the 2013 state championship. In 2014, Loniewski, Skellett, Katie Minnich, and Roxanne Griffore became state title–holders in the 200-yard medley relay; they were coached by Shannon Dunworth, who led Mercy to six state championships between 2004 and 2015. (Courtesy of the *Detroit Free Press*; photograph by Kirthmon F. Dozier.)

The Marlins won their 28th straight Catholic High School League title in swimming in 2018. They are pictured celebrating their victory with another trophy after defeating runner-up Bloomfield Hills Marian High by nearly 200 points. The Marlins, coached by Mike Venos (standing at far left), finished the season by winning the 2018 Michigan Division 1 state championship. Mercy swimmers also captured the state title in 2019—the school's 11th state swim and dive championship win.

At the 2020–2021 state championship meet, Mercy diver Ciara McCliment ('21) won the state title. She signed to dive for the University of Illinois Chicago. Greta Gidley ('21) was the state champion in two events, winning titles in the 200-yard individual medley and 500-yard freestyle. She signed with the University of Michigan. The Marlins finished the season as runners-up to champion Ann Arbor Pioneer High. Gidley is pictured holding the state runners-up trophy with her teammates.

In 2019, Mercy High won its first state volleyball championship, powered in part by the talent of Jessica "Jess" Mruzik, pictured above holding the 2019–2020 Gatorade National Player of the Year trophy. After the 2019 volleyball season was over, Mruzik graduated early from Mercy to enroll at the University of Michigan on a volleyball scholarship. She was also voted on to the All-American Volleyball 1st Team and named Michigan's Miss Volleyball. In the below image, Mruzik leads Mercy High past archrival Marian High in an October 2018 game. (Below, courtesy of Hometown Life; photograph by Dan Dean.)

Maddy Doyle was the engine of the 2010 Mercy Volleyball team, which was the state runner-up and the Catholic League champ. Above, she learns that she won the coveted Miss Volleyball award, as selected by high school team coaches, during a surprise assembly at Mercy High in 2011. (Courtesy of the *Detroit Free Press*; photograph by Julian Gonzalez.)

Even in a pandemic-shortened season, Mercy girls shined on the volleyball court. Standout Julia Bishop ('21) was named Miss Volleyball Michigan for 2020. She is pictured at center holding the Miss Volleyball trophy. This was the second year in a row that the prestigious honor went to a Marlin. Bishop had more than 5,000 assists as a Marlin volleyball player. Standing to the left of Bishop is Charli Atiemo ('21), who was also a finalist for the award.

Mercy High has won two state basketball championships. The team lost three state championship games in a row in 1974, 1975, and 1976. In the above photograph, coach Larry Baker, who was also an English teacher, discusses strategy with players huddled around him. In 1977, Mercy girls defeated Detroit Mumford High 63–52 to win their first state title. Mercy girls are shown celebrating in the photograph at left, led by Laura Zwiller in the foreground. (Above, courtesy of Mary Pat Conen Hammell; left, courtesy of Larry Baker.)

In 2016, Mercy hosted a reunion for the 1977 and 1982 championship basketball squads. In 1982, Mercy was a surprise contender, and the team faced four-time defending state champions Flint Northern in the final game. Down 19 points with 17 minutes left, Mercy coach Larry Baker switched strategies to deploy his diamond press. Flint Northern made turnover after turnover, Mercy player Amanda Rosowski made six steals, Amy DeMattia scored six straight points, and Annette Ruggiero made a key steal to record a 61–58 upset. Among the reunion attendees was 1977 team captain Diane Dietz. Dietz is considered one of the best women's basketball players to come out of Michigan. At the University of Michigan (UM), she set the university's single-game scoring record with 45 points in a 1982 game—a record that remained unbroken until 2018. She holds UM's second all-time scoring record with 2,076 points. She was named an All-American basketball player and was the first women's basketball player inducted into the University of Michigan Hall of Honor. For the last 10 years, she has worked as the chief communications officer for the Big Ten conference. Assistant coach Mike King (at far left in the first row) and coach Larry Baker (at far right in the first row) coached both teams. The 1977 squad in the front row included, from left to right, Carolyn Chapman Arbour, Gretchen Hart Larges, Lisa Morris, Dietz, Lynn Yadach-Blakey, Suzanne Brown, and Nancy Malone Sullivan; 1977 team member Patricia Schneider is at farthest right in the second row. The 1982 team members pictured in the second row are, from left to right, Kathleen Kirwan McMillen, Mimi Bosco Sale, Peggy Kelley, Lisa Yezbick, Sarah Basford, Tracey Smith Roberts, and Terri Nalodka Murray. (Courtesy of the *Detroit Free Press*; photograph by John Froehlich.)

Alexis Roberts ('21) drives the lane in a March 10, 2020, game against Detroit Renaissance High School. The squad, which did not have a single senior on the roster, won the Catholic League title and finished the season with a 20–4 record. The COVID-19 pandemic led to the suspension of school sports in mid-March 2020. As a result, the state girls' basketball playoffs were cancelled. (Courtesy of the *Oakland Press*; photograph by Ken Swart.)

Senior cocaptain Taylor Jones helped power Mercy to a 20–5 record in the 2014–2015 season. She scored a career high 37 points in a state district championship quarterfinal. The team, coached by Gary Morris, also won a state district title with a 60–43 win over Detroit Mumford. In the 2014 Catholic League A-B Title game, Jones stole the ball from a Marian High player with 4.2 seconds on the clock for the win.

Boardercross, also known as SBX or snowboardcross, is the newest winter sport offered at Mercy High. Credit Samantha Fee (at center in the above image), who won an individual state title at the Michigan High School Snowboard Association championships in 2020, her senior year. In ninth grade, Fee made a proposal to the school's sports department to form a squad. It was not until Fee's senior year that the sport became official. At right is the 2020 Marlins boardercross team. From left to right are Sofia Zestos, Sophie Chiminski, Isabelle Werner, Mae Korte, Bryce Gordon, Fee, and Bailey Marino; coach Andrew Fee stands behind them. (Both, courtesy of Samantha Fee.)

Cathleen Kowalski Maes ('05) is Mercy's most decorated bowler. In her sophomore season, Cathleen led the team to the Catholic League Championship in its first year of competition. She was also crowned the individual champion. Her 200 average in her senior year led to her receiving the Golden Pin Award and being named to the All-State Dream Team as one of the five best bowlers in Michigan. She was awarded a scholarship to bowl at Minnesota State University, Mankato, and her team qualified for the NCAA championship twice in her four years at the school. Since returning to Michigan, she has established herself as a top bowler. She won the Metro Detroit U.S. Bowling Congress Queens Championship in 2018 and its Tournament of Champions in 2019. She helps coach the Mercy bowling squad alongside her mother, math teacher Vicky Bunetta Kowalski. (Courtesy of the *Detroit Free Press*; photograph by William Archie.)

Mercy's bowling team has won nine Catholic League championships—in 2003, 2008, 2009, 2011, 2012, 2014, 2019, 2020, and 2021. Here is the team that claimed the crown in 2011. Kneeling is Brittany Jones, and standing are, from left to right, Kathleen Abenes, Eleanor Carey, Erica Canavan, Jasmine Wehr, Maria Walawender, and Leah Harlan.

Mercy math teacher Vicky Bunetta Kowalski, pictured at right, shows off the 1999 state golf championship trophy. The Marlins won another state title in 2001. The highly honored coach will begin her 42nd season at Mercy in fall 2021. The Marlins golf team has won 17 Catholic League titles.

It is rare for a golfer to get a hole in one in a lifetime on the greens, but Marlin varsity golfer Chloe Vig ('23) recorded two in one week! Her first ace occurred on September 24, 2020, on South Hole 5 at the Detroit Golf Club. She did it again at the Catholic High School League Championship on the same course on September 28, 2020, when she swung for another on South Hole 17. (Courtesy of Kim Vig.)

Professional golfer Meg Mallon (above, class of 1981) was on the first Mercy High golf squad, which was established by coach Vicky Bunetta Kowalski in 1979. Mallon joined the Ladies Pro Golf Association (LPGA) tour in 1987. Ten years out of Mercy, Mallon won the US Women's Open in 1991, and she won it again in 2004. In 1991, the Golf Writers Association of America named her Female Player of the Year. She is recognized as the most successful golf professional to hail from Michigan. For 20 years, Mallon headlined a Mercy fundraising golf tournament named after her. Below, at the 1998 Meg Mallon Golf Outing, she is second from right. To the left of her are Mercy principal Sr. Regina Marie Doelker and John Mallon, the golfer's brother. At far right is WDIV-TV sports announcer Steve Garagiola. (Above, courtesy of the *Detroit Free Press*; photograph by Julian Gonzalez.)

Mercy's lacrosse team has advanced to the state Final Four 10 times since 2000, including in 2021. The Marlins were state runners-up in 2002 and 2008. In the image at right, senior goalie Hannah Cohen ('16) stands ready in a match against Cranbrook-Kingswood. (Courtesy of the *Oakland Press*; photograph by Ken Swart.)

Jillian Smith ('21) dominated in lacrosse at Mercy like no other player. She was named to the Under Armour All-American Midwest team and selected to the National Lacrosse Classic All-American and All-Star squads. For Mercy, she set 16 state records in her freshman year and 12 as a sophomore. Her junior season was cut short by the COVID-19 pandemic. In her senior year, the lacrosse team advanced to the state semifinals. One of her records includes most points in a single game. She is pictured below signing to play at the University of Michigan.

Some members of the first Mercy ice hockey teams learned how to skate during practices, as ice hockey was a fledgling sport for girls in the early 2000s. At the November 2005 match pictured above, Mercy's Maura Gregory ('06; center) is shown breaking away from the Northville High defense. Below, Jacqueline Roberge ('08) takes a break during practice in February 2006; the team that year included a goalie and four ninth-graders who had not skated before. (Both, courtesy of the *Detroit Free Press*; above, photograph by Jerry S. Mendoza; below, photograph by William Archie.)

Today, the Mercy ice hockey team is far removed from its wobbly early years. Mercy has won five state championships in the Michigan Metro Girls' Hockey League. The Marlins reigned as champs in 2013, 2015, 2016, 2017, and 2019. Above, the 2015 state champions celebrate. Below, members of the 2019 state champion team clasp the championship trophy. They are, from left to right, Sydney Takla ('20), Grace Nieto ('21), Libby Bartels ('19), Abbey Roegner ('19), and goalie Daria Rorick ('22). Bartels was named Miss Hockey for the 2019 season. (Below, courtesy of StudentandAthlete.org.)

Marlins Christina Nypayer (No. 5) and Shannon Moore (No. 8) fight for the ball with a Stoney Creek High School player during a 2006 invitational. (Courtesy of the *Detroit Free Press*; photograph by Eric Seals.)

Mercy's Macey Earle (No. 11) gets a foot on the ball during a game against Farmington High School in April 2019. (Courtesy of the *Oakland Press*; photograph by Ken Swart.)

During the match against Farmington High in April 2019, there were moments of glee when Mercy scored two goals. Above, Lindsey Lukomski (right) congratulates a fellow Mercy player, and below, Mercy teammates share high fives. The game ended in a 2–2 tie. Mercy's soccer team made it to the state semifinals in 1990. Mercy has won six district championships—in 1988, 1990, 1991, 1992, 2007, and 2012. (Both, courtesy of the *Oakland Press*; photograph by Ken Swart.)

Mercy skier Denise Hartsock ('98) conquered the girls' slalom at Nubs Nub near Petoskey during the state skiing championship in 1998, the same year the team won a Catholic League division title. The Marlin ski squad has won six regional championships. (Courtesy of the *Detroit Free Press*; photograph by Craig Porter.)

From the first days the school was open, Mercy girls enjoyed equestrian pursuits. The equestrian team won a regional championship in 2014 and district reserve championships in 2014 and 2019 through the Michigan Interscholastic Horsemanship Association. In 2020, the equestrian team won district and regional reserve championships.

In 2005, Mercy won the Catholic League cross-country championships—the school's 13th title since 1977. Members of that team are pictured above. Below, cross-country runner Lily Fromm ('22) strides for Mercy in a meet as a ninth-grader in October 2018. (Below, courtesy of StudentandAthlete.org.)

What a wind-up! Mercy's Andrea Elmore (above) unleashes a pitch against Macomb Dakota High on June 16, 2016, at the Michigan High School Athletic Association Division 1 softball championship at Michigan State University, where Mercy clinched its first state softball championship with a 4–2 victory—and the Marlins celebrated with gusto (below). Prior to the championship victory, the Marlins had finished second in the 2002 title game. (Both, courtesy of the *Detroit Free Press*; photograph by Salwan Georges.)

After the pandemic cancelled the 2020 season, the Marlins returned to the softball field in 2021 in spectacular fashion. The squad won the Catholic League title and mowed down its opponents all the way to the Michigan Athletic Association Division 1 semifinals. Softball standout Maggie Murphy ('21), above, was safe as she slid into home in a victorious 14–4 regional championship game against Clarkston High on June 12, 2021. The team's season ended at the state semifinals with a 9–5 defeat against Allen Park High. This was the Marlins' best run since the Mercy team won the 2016 softball title. (Both, courtesy of the *Oakland Press*; photograph by Matthew B. Mowery.)

It's relay time! Wearing Mercy maroon and gold, Kristina Bell ('07; near the left side of the image) and Ashley Terry ('08; foreground) prepare for the relay handoff. Mercy's track and field team won 14 Catholic League championships from 1978 through 2009. The squad added a 15th title in 2021, when Mackenzie Sullivan ('21) set a school record in the 300-meter hurdles and raced on the 4-by-800-meter relay team with Mary Shah, Kate Heaman, and Maddy Kennedy as they set a new school record.

Amanda Herdoiza ('20) sends the ball flying in this 2018 tennis match. The Mercy tennis team won three consecutive state regional championships in 2017, 2018, and 2019. Mercy was the runner-up for the 2013 state championship. (Courtesy of StudentandAthlete.org.)

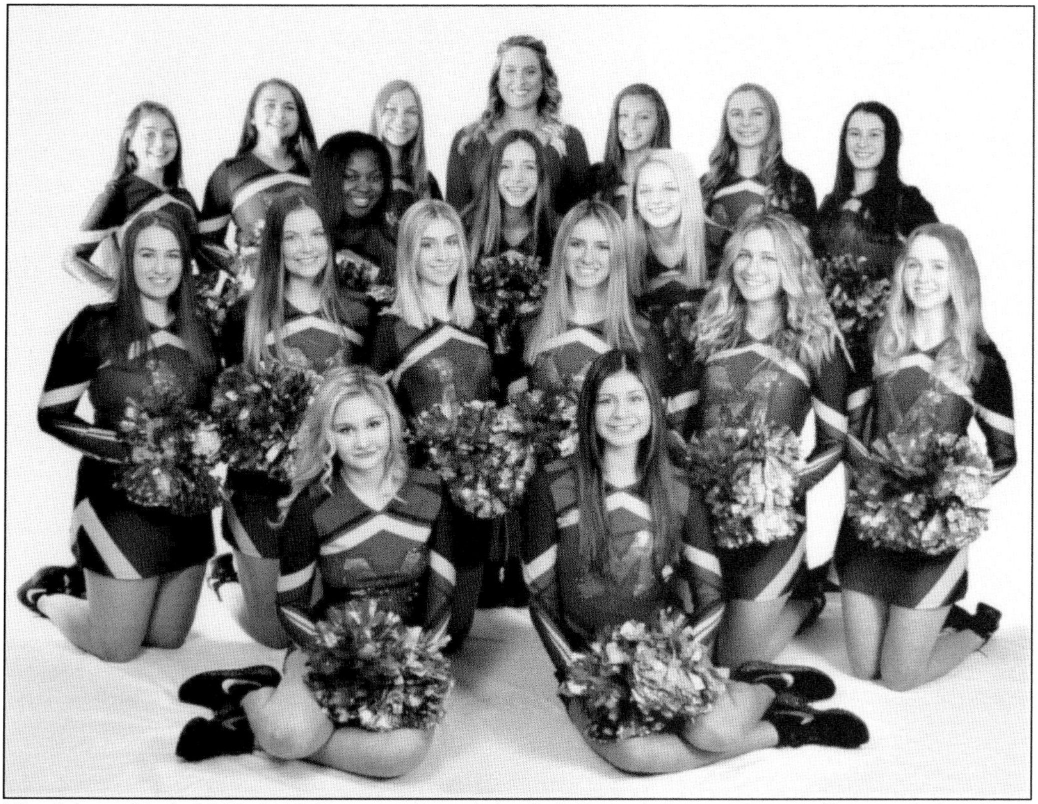

The Mercy High 2018–2019 Pompon Squad dazzled. From left to right are (first row) Carolynn Schuring and Madelyn McSweeney; (second row) Brooke Hegarty, Bridget D'Amore, Joanie Langan, Ashley Doyle, Rachel Pierson, and Kieran Neaton; (third row) Qeren Blakey, Gabby Jeannotte, and Lila Bidoul; (fourth row) Andrea Andres, Ary Martinez, Sophia Herman, coach Kirstie Liakos, Grace O'Dea, Justina Bloch, and Madelyn Leiter. In the 2019–2020 season, the squad was a runner-up at the state championship competition. No matter the sport, there is a lot to cheer about if one is a Mercy Marlin.

These are the members of the of the 2017–2018 ice-skating squad. Pictured here are, from left to right, (first row) Selina George, Mary Grace Piotrowski, Sophia Lyons, Isabelle Fanning, and Jenna Bratke; (second row) Alexa Zydeck, Alexa Rybicki, Tia Hockenhull, coach Michelle Sibley, Jo Thompson, Avery Swickard, and Corinne Fereshetian. Mercy won state championships in ice-skating in 2002, 2003, and 2007.

The Mercy High Dance Team made it to the finals at a national competition hosted by the University Dance Association in February 2020. From left to right are Sophia Moussa, Kendra Fereshetian, Kinsey Burr, Alexa Fras, Brooke Heery, Katherine Gutowsky, Keira Logan, Claire Harris, Calla Place, Emily Casalou, and Anna Buckman.

This trio of Mercy swimmers is bursting with school pride. From left to right are Hannah Knoop ('14), Annie Valentine ('13), and Erin Judd ('16).

Longtime Mercy High athletics director Nancy Malinowski is announcing the winner of the annual Garn Griffin Athletic Award, which is given to top student athletes, for the 2013–2014 school year. Sam Bauer (left), a basketball and softball standout, and Jordan Ewald, softball team leader, were the honorees. Malinowski has twice been honored by the Catholic High School League with the prestigious Tom Kelly Athletic Director of the Year Award for good sportsmanship.

Pictured above are some of the Mercy seniors who signed college letters of intent in 2020. They are, from left to right, (first row) Mackenzie Sullivan, track at University of Pittsburgh; Peyton Smith, lacrosse at Northern Michigan University; and Ciara McCliment, diving at the University of Illinois Chicago; (second row) Maya Goudeseune, soccer at University of Kentucky; Greta Gidley, swimming at University of Michigan; and Samantha Diaz, swimming at University of Wyoming. Mercy athletes are always encouraged by the support of the fuzzy and fierce Marlin mascot (left). It is considered an honor for a Mercy girl to perform as the costumed Marlin.

Four

Mercy Moments to Shine

Mercy High is a mosaic of faces and talents. Mercy students come from more than 60 communities across metropolitan Detroit. The school's students identify themselves as having the following backgrounds: 60 percent Caucasian, 11 percent Middle Eastern/Chaldean, 10 percent African American, 4 percent Asian/Indian, 4 percent Hispanic, and 3 percent multiracial. The school highlights its diversity during an annual Ethnic Bazaar, where students celebrate with dances and performances that reflect their backgrounds.

Students pray at a courtyard statue honoring the Blessed Virgin Mary. The marble statue came from the old Detroit Mount Carmel Hospital that was once operated by Sisters of Mercy. Catholic teachings are part of the four-year curriculum. Mercy accepts girls from all faiths. Students are required to take four years of classes in religion and spirituality and attend scheduled Masses. A daily prayer is shared over the school's broadcast system and emailed to Mercy families.

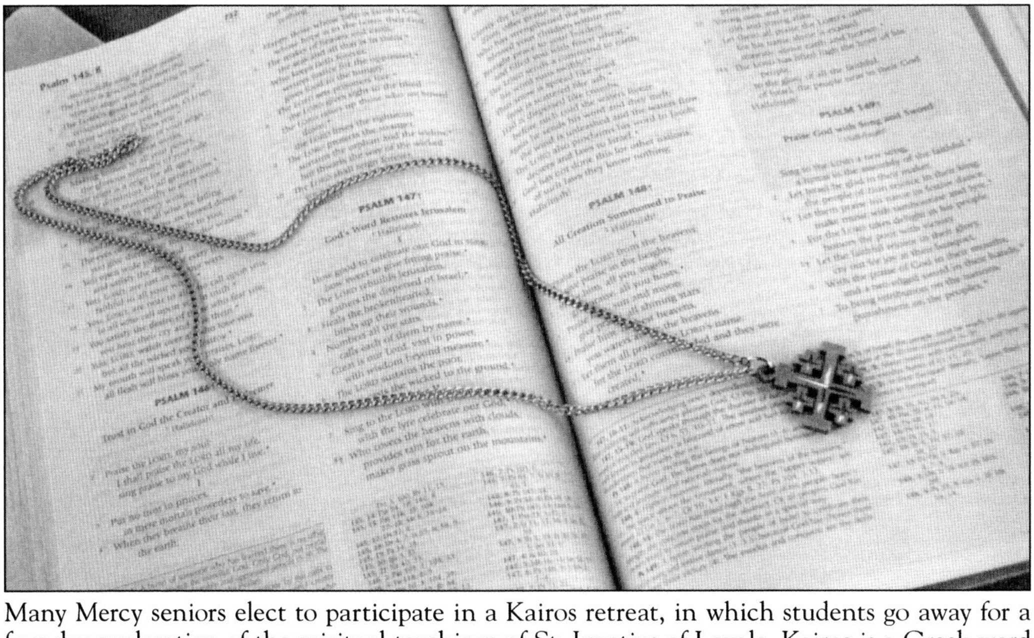

Many Mercy seniors elect to participate in a Kairos retreat, in which students go away for a four-day exploration of the spiritual teachings of St. Ignatius of Loyola. Kairos is a Greek word roughly meaning an opportunity to take action. Each participant receives a Kairos cross necklace, as pictured here.

Seniors from religion teacher Ann Lusch's prayer and spirituality class gather in the chapel for a discussion on discernment in March 2020. Sometimes, evaluating what decision to make starts with a simple list of pros and cons—and a prayer. Pictured here are, from left to right, Isabella Whitton, Bella Aprilliano, Mariel Kraim, and Amanda Herdoiza.

The Mercy High labyrinth is designed to provide students with an avenue for contemplative prayer. A walk in the labyrinth is called a "purgation," according to the Mercy High Campus Ministry Office. Such a walk can distract those tracing its circles from their everyday stress and concerns.

The members of the Mercy Robotics team call themselves the Riveters in tribute to the iconic Rosie the Riveter, who symbolized the women who took on factory jobs during World War II. The team has won state and national awards.

Mercy's Right to Life Club makes an annual bus journey to Washington, DC, for the March for Life demonstration against abortion. The rally is held every January around the time of the anniversary of the US Supreme Court decision in 1973 that legalized abortion, which is opposed by the Roman Catholic Church. Here, the students gather at the Jefferson Memorial.

"Make A Difference Day" is part of the autumn Spirit Week events. Much can be accomplished when over 700 Mercy students and staff undertake community projects over the course of three hours. In the below photograph, Mercy girls are at Detroit civil rights and social services agency Focus: HOPE helping to pack and distribute food for low-income customers. The school notes that, "Our volunteer program promotes the school's philosophy of learning to care and serve, and how to put our Mercy Values into action. How to be the Hands of God to one another! How to be a Woman Who Makes a Difference."

Mercy's Anne Kator and Jesse LaRochelle, a University of Detroit Jesuit High student, are shown making a stunning entrance at the 2006 Mercy High prom at the Roostertail on the Detroit River. The high school sweethearts eventually married each other.

In 2020, Mercy High renovated lobby space into a tea room adjacent to the newly updated Marlin Shop. Catherine's Tea Parlor is named after the Venerable Catherine McAuley, who founded the Sisters of Mercy in Dublin in 1831 and enjoyed afternoon tea. The stained-glass window is an artifact from Mercy's first campus in Detroit and links the former and current schools in the spirit of McAuley.

Sr. Regina Marie Doelker (left) welcomes Emma Caverlry to Mercy High School after the student enrolled following the disruption caused in New Orleans by Hurricane Katrina in 2005. Sister Regina's Mercy career enveloped the lives of thousands of Mercy High students. She was a 1956 alumna who entered the congregation, taught math at Mercy from 1964 to 1974, was school principal from 1986 to 2001, and served as president of Mercy president from 2002 to 2010. She died in August 2019 at age 81.

Carolyn Witte ('67) has been a Mercy student, alumna, parent, English teacher, and principal. She credits English teacher Louise Scudlo for inspiring her to become a teacher. She became the first layperson to be named principal of Mercy High. She served in that role from 2001 to 2017, capping 42 years of working service to the school. Witte and Sr. Regina Marie Doelker both have endowed scholarship funds at the school.

Dr. Cheryl Delaney Kreger, EdD, has guided Mercy High as the school's president since 2010. A 1966 alumna, she taught special education and held several top administrative positions, including associate superintendent, with Dearborn Public Schools. In 2007, she became the Okemos Public Schools superintendent. Most recently, she was named a *Crain's Detroit Business* 2019 Notable Woman in Educational Leadership. In every public address she delivers, Kreger makes a point of invoking the name and legacy of the Venerable Catherine McAuley, the Irish foundress of the Sisters of Mercy. Dr. Kreger is pictured with Tyler Parlor (right), a former business office accounting assistant and 2014 alumna.

Mary Harkness, who graduated from Mercy High, has been a fixture at the school's front desk and celebrated her 50-year work anniversary in 2021. Her mother worked at the original Mercy High School in Detroit. On this day, she was signing in visitors who were attending the school's Heart of Mercy Mass in March 2020. (Photograph by Diane Weiss.)

Karli Winfrey ('15) was a Mercy High senior in the fall of 2014 when she emailed Oprah Winfrey, a distant cousin, asking the superstar to speak at the all-girls school. "I told her about Mercy . . . how we really respect Oprah because she's an icon for women's empowerment," the student told the *Detroit Free Press*. Oprah responded by inviting Mercy's 222 seniors (plus one guest per student) to her "The Life You Want" extravaganza event in the Detroit area. (Courtesy of the *Detroit Free Press*; photograph by Diane Weiss.)

Michelle McCarthy ('10; standing) won a State of Michigan award in 2008 for her website, Geek Girls, which focused on young women who like technology and computer work. To her right is Taylor Moore. (Courtesy of the *Detroit Free Press*; photograph by Patricia Beck.)

Isadora Baughman ('16; left) and Hadley Hrdlicka ('16) were adept at using their Apple iPads to enhance the Mercy curriculum. In November 2013, Apple awarded a "Distinguished School" designation to Mercy, making it one of only three schools in Michigan to receive the award. Baughman, for example, displayed technological creativity when she produced a video of a speech with sound effects and images. (Courtesy of the *Detroit Free Press*; photograph by Eric Seals.)

Mercy girls studying journalism are gatherers of multimedia news. *Newsprint* is produced by a class of juniors and seniors who have completed a challenging journalism course. Mercy's *Newsprint* student newspaper is published monthly. Its round-the-clock online product is called Newsprint Now. From 2006 to 2020, former *Detroit News* journalist Lynn Waldsmith taught journalism at Mercy and oversaw the *Newsprint* staff and production. In seven years at the *Detroit News*, Waldsmith covered banking, economic development, parenting, and education issues. *Newsprint* staffers typically win numerous awards each year from the Michigan Interscholastic Press Association for their work in photography, writing, and design.

The Mercy Mimes troupe was established in 1991 by drama teacher Kathy Sill as an extracurricular activity. Students are eligible to try out after taking drama or oral interpretation classes. The troupe is a staple at Mercy functions as well as many community events.

In the music industry, she's known as the talented singer-songwriter Mozella. To Mercy girls, she's Maureen McDonald, class of 1999. She cowrote Miley Cyrus's *Billboard* chart-topper "Wrecking Ball" and songs for the Jonas Brothers, Keith Urban, Kelly Clarkson, and One Direction. She cowrote 11 of 19 tracks on Madonna's 2015 album *Rebel Heart*. Her own releases include *MoZella*, *Belle Isle*, and a collaboration with legendary Motown songwriter Brian Holland called *Mozella: The Brian Holland Sessions*. On her website (mozellamusic.com), she gives the following advice: "Stay open and keep creating no matter what. Songs are human experiences. So be human and write about it." (Courtesy of No Expectations Music; photograph by Nick Spanos.)

As a ninth-grader at Mercy, Susan Smith won a national art award after taking art classes. After her 1984 graduation, she became an art teacher, joining the Mercy staff in 1990. In February 2020, she was awarded the Michigan Region Scholastic Inspiring Educator Award.

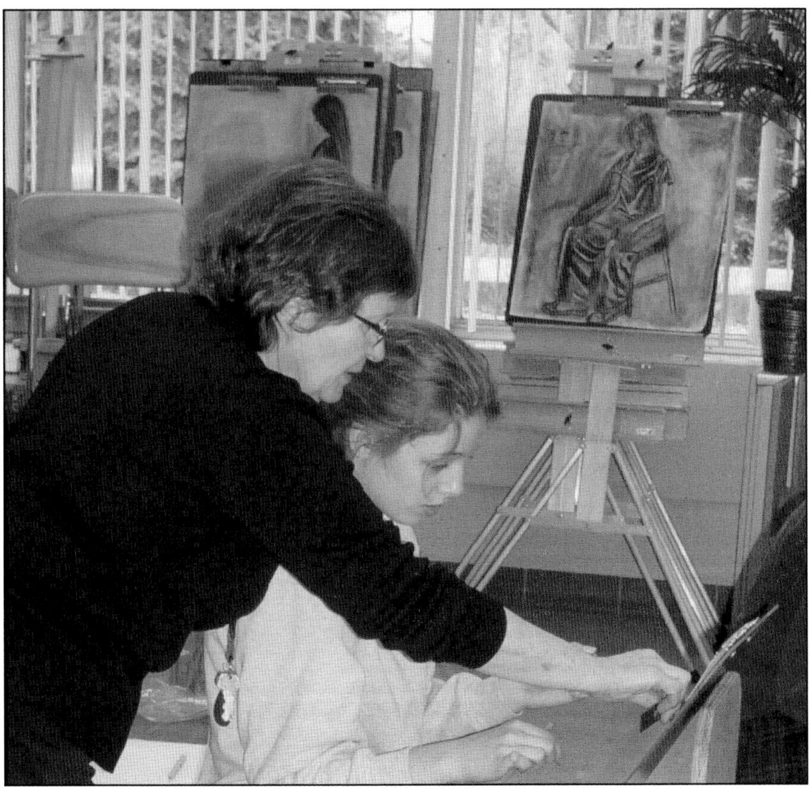

Art teacher Carol Rife, who retired in 2021, gives tips on drawing in charcoal. Rife also taught ceramic arts. Mercy's ceramics studio is equipped with 11 potter's wheels, a slab roller, a clay extruder, and 4 ceramics kilns.

This self-portrait of Mercy High student and artist Brittani Czarnecki ('05) was included in her portfolio, which earned the coveted Gold Key in the regional Scholastic Art & Writing Awards in 2005. About half of Mercy students take an art class each year.

These Mercy art students put on their own show in the hallway. From left to right are (first row) Phelan Storck ('20), Emma Engquist ('20), and Madeline Briggs ('21); (second row) Angela Rea ('20) and Grace Kelley ('20). Mercy offers dozens of courses in varied art media. Mercy has 4 studio classrooms, 2 computer labs, 26 looms, a ceramics studio, and a jewelry studio.

Kathy Sill (second from left) started teaching at Mercy High in 1967 as Kathy Duross. She established the Mercy Mimes and coached the school's forensics squad. Most memorably, she directed the school's musicals and plays. She is pictured here in 2014 on the day she received the Heart of Mercy award. All three Mercy students in this photograph hailed from Asia and were being hosted at the Sill home. They are, from left to right, Yayun (Helen) Zheng ('17), from China; Jinghan (Molane) Hu ('16), from China; and HyeJeong (Blair) Cha ('16), from Korea.

When English teacher Kathy Duross met speech teacher Ron Sill at Mercy High, an enduring creative collaboration ensued. He served as the theater technical director and stage crew guru from 1970 to 2011. She directed 55 theatrical productions over her Mercy career and founded the Mercy Mimes. Their three daughters are Mercy alumnae. Amy Sill Iacobell ('93) was a school admissions codirector from 2016 to 2021, Amanda Sill Fylan ('95) worked as Mercy's admissions director from 2000 to 2004, and Anne Sill MacDougall ('98) taught speech and drama from 2011 to 2019. Kathy and Ron chaperoned the Mercy Christmas Dance in 2014, as they've done for decades. They both taught at Mercy for 40 years each. Even after retiring, Ron worked on Mercy productions through 2018, and Kathy directed the Mercy Mimes until 2021.

In the fall of 2010, Mercy staged *Little Women.* The cast members pictured above are, from left to right, (first row) Jane Huffman, Sarah Kmiecik, Anna Siebert, Caroline Powers, and Kelly Redmond; (second row) Margaret Malaney, Bridget Johnson, Emily Shimskey, and Rachel Anctil. Below is a quick-stepping dance scene from the 2013 spring musical, *Annie Get Your Gun.*

BASE (Black Awareness Society for Education) is a Mercy club open to all that has a goal to "unite and educate students of various backgrounds on issues and events that occur in the world and which impact racial harmony." BASE events during the school year include presenting a Black History Month program, as these Mercy students did in 2020. Many members also perform during the school's annual Ethnic Bazaar.

Mercy's annual Ethnic Bazaar is a kaleidoscope of talent and ethnic pride. These students are of Middle Eastern descent and are performing a dance with ancient roots that stretch back to Iraq and a part of that country that is home to the Iraqi Catholics known as Chaldeans.

Mercy students who train and compete in Irish step dancing often perform at the Ethnic Bazaar. Students also perform Bollywood-like dances to celebrate family ties to India, as well as folk dances from European countries.

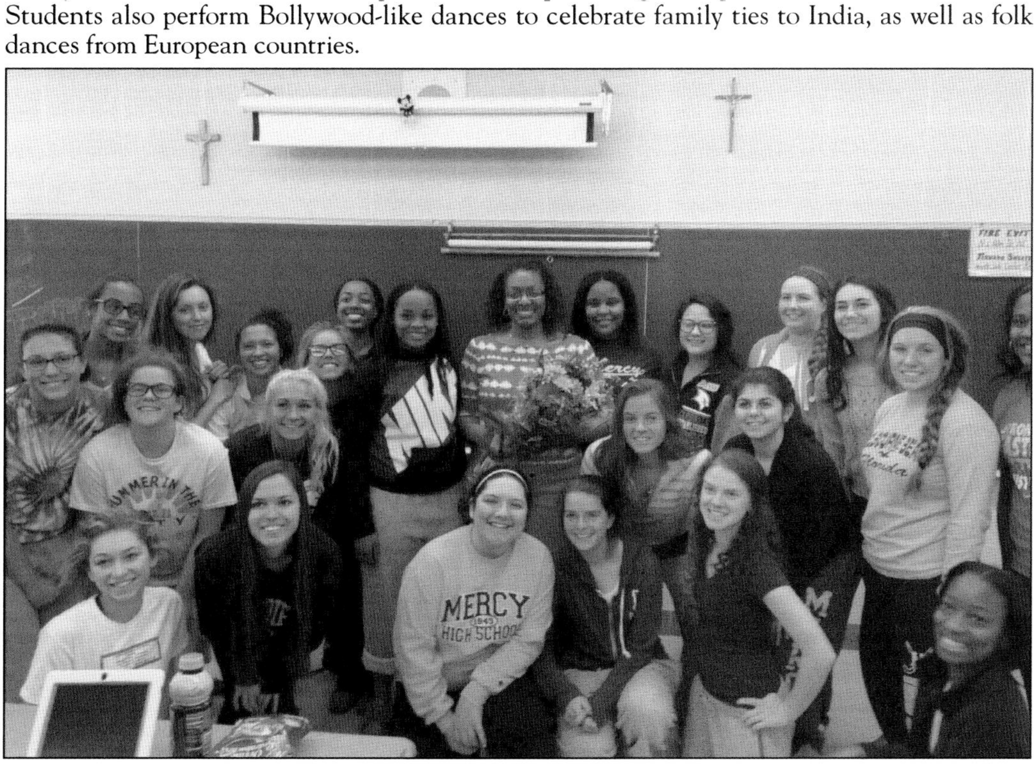

The 2014 Mercy Teacher of the Year, Eleasha Tarplin, is holding a bouquet as she stands among some of her students. Since the 2014–2015 school year, Tarplin has been dean of student affairs, overseeing all the nonacademic programs and extracurricular activities.

Lauren Lake, a.k.a. Lauren Howard ('86), is comfortable and authoritative in the spotlight. From 2013 to 2020, the lawyer and legal analyst probed family dynamics on the nationally syndicated *Lauren Lake's Paternity Court*, which won a Daytime Emmy Award in 2019. Here, she is featured on a WXYZ-TV newscast on Nov. 28, 2016. A onetime Mercyaire, she has sung background vocals for Mary J. Blige, Jay-Z, Dr. Dre, and Snoop Dogg. She also hosted episodes of HGTV's *Spice Up My Kitchen* from May 2007 to 2009. (Courtesy of WXYZ-TV.)

Many of Mercy's 16,000 alumnae have distinguished themselves in the field of law. When the school held a Law Affinity Event in 2019, these Mercy grads shared their experiences as jurists. Pictured here are, from left to right, (first row) the honorable Victoria Valentine ('89) and Kathleen Ryan ('87); (second row) the honorable Julie McDonald ('87), Roberta Orr Archer ('88), and Diane Dickow D'Agostini ('80). Orr Archer is a Detroit 36th District Court judge. The others are sitting judges in Oakland County. In June 2021, Pres. Joe Biden nominated alumna Jia Cobb ('98), a Harvard Law School graduate and former trial attorney at the Public Defender Service for Washington, DC, to the US District Court for the District of Columbia.

The James sisters attended Mercy High and started the successful organic cold-pressed juice company Drought in 2011. Drought eclectic elixirs—juice Green No. 1 blends chard, cabbage, apple, celery, kale, and lemon—are available at retailers locally and in dozens of states. Pictured at the Royal Oak store in 2015 are, from left to right, Caitlin James ('02), Jenny James ('05), Jessie James (who attended Mercy for three years), and Julie James ('00). (Courtesy of the *Detroit Free Press*, photograph by Mandi Wright.)

Mercy holds a reunion weekend each September for classes celebrating milestones ranging from 5- to 50-year anniversaries. The class of 1989 assembled for this reunion. "Mercy's 16,000 alumnae are a strong sisterhood and the heart and soul of Mercy High School today. Whether they graduated from Our Lady of Mercy on Outer Drive in Detroit or Mercy High School in Farmington Hills, they share the same values and are 'Women who make a difference,'" says Mercy president Dr. Cheryl Delaney Kreger ('66), who attended the school at both locations.

Sisters of Mercy who taught at the school enjoy an evening at the school's annual auction. From farthest left are, going around the table clockwise, Srs. Jane Mackowiak, Marianne Bennett, Camille Kelley, Mary Timothy Brown, Jane Fox, Elizabeth Mary Burns, Nancy Thompson, Mary Joel Zobro, and Theresa Blaquiere.

Mercy president Dr. Cheryl Delaney Kreger leads a ceremonial groundbreaking ceremony in 2018 to expand a parking lot for the North Campus sports fields at Mercy High. Pictured here are (left to right) Connie Demkowicz, Rita Dilworth Lewry ('77), Nancy Auffenberg, and Kreger. Demkowicz, Lewry, and Auffenberg all have daughters who are Mercy graduates.

Class of 2020 seniors were honored at a Mercy Alumnae Association lunch. From the left foreground, going clockwise around the table are Soli Evans, Katherine Broderick, Julia Coffman, Anthonia Ahaiwe, Lily Beasley, Sandy DiPonio ('87), Samantha Shea, Lauren Piziali, Annabel Shammami, and Aaryn Harris.

Sr. Nancy Thompson ('50) addresses an alumnae event. Not only is she an alumna, but she has also taught at Mercy, served as an assistant principal, and was Mercy's fourth principal. She was the second Mercy alumna to serve as the school principal. In recent years, she has worked with Mercy's advancement office and as the school's archivist; she was also Mercy's interim president from 2001 to 2002. To the right is Mercy alumnae director Laura Merritt Everett ('98).

Every fall, Spirit Week brings zaniness and competition to Mercy. The freshman, sophomore, junior, and senior classes compete against each other in games. There is also a fierce tug-of-war between a select crew of seniors and the faculty, as shown at left. Below, class of 2020 members unleashed their creativity with chalk art drawn on school parking spaces in an effort to raise money for senior activities.

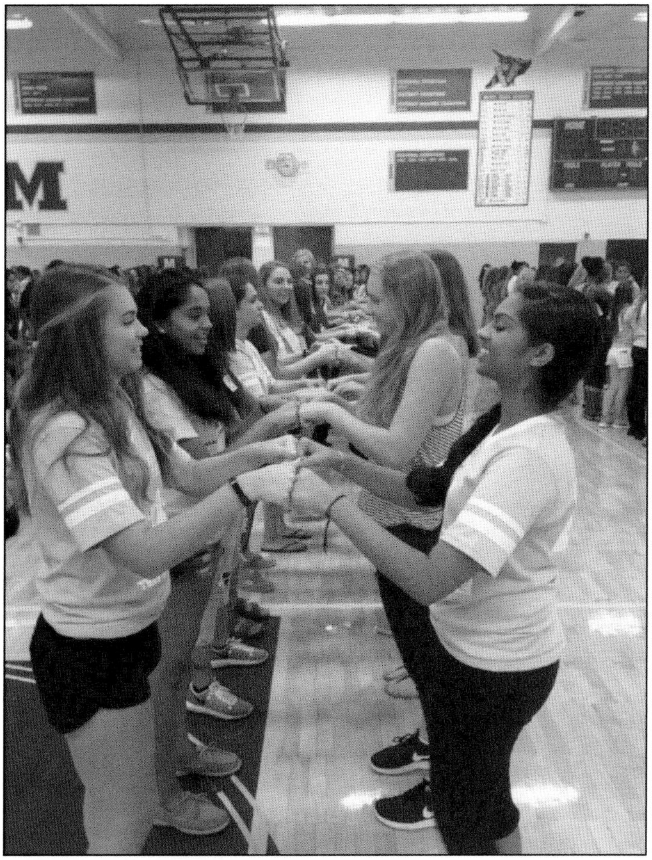

The Link Crew program at Mercy High pairs ninth graders with Link Leaders—students from upper grades who help orient and befriend a crew of new students. The Link Crew experience is the key component of Freshwoman Welcome Day Orientation, but the Link Leader also stays in touch with her "crew" to help them transition into high school and the Mercy experience. Its faculty leaders are ninth-grade counselor Trish Brown and teacher Sara McGavin. The Link Program traces its roots to the Big Sister/ Little Sister program familiar to many Mercy alumnae.

Lisa Ludwinski (right) is a 2002 alumna who has earned national recognition for Sister Pie bakery, which she opened on Detroit's east side in 2015. She has been a three-time finalist for the James Beard Award, which recognizes excellence among chefs, bakers, and cooks. In this fall 2019 photograph, she poses in her store, Mercy coffee mug in hand, with Sister Pie employee Nyah Williams, a 2020 Mercy graduate. (Courtesy of Lisa Ludwinski.)

Mercy High's pastoral minister Judi Griggs-Dennis has arranged service trips for Mercy students to take during Easter break for more than 20 years. In 2012, Mercy seniors helped build houses for Habitat for Humanity in Kentucky. From left to right are Colette Berg, Ellen Lezotte, Jasmine Wehr, and Natalie Diehl.

Mercy High never had lockers lining its hallways. Instead, lockers were in the basement, but students usually lugged around all their books and outerwear rather than going downstairs. In 2020, the basement was converted to the M-Zone, an athletic training facility, in memory of Sr. Regina Marie Doelker ('56).

When Spanish teacher Vita Sinutko (seated, second from left) retired in 2016, other retired teachers gathered at Mercy to offer their retirement tips. Seated from left to right are (first row) Sr. Nancy Thompson, Sinutko, Kay Dingeman, Sr. Regina Marie Doelker, Lorrie Kusch, Mike Gruber, and Kathy Kitzmann; (second row) John Eschelman, Sue Noll, Sr. Marianne Bennett, John Gernacy, George Wright, Tony Scalzi, Judy Pauley, Sherri Howard, Fran Mika, Carolyn Witte, Judy Ewald, and Peter McGrane.

In 2016, Sommer Woods, a 1995 graduate, was honored as Alumna of the Year and addressed the crowd at the annual Mercy Tea for Tuition. She was the first Black woman to be honored with the award. Woods was the vice president of marketing and communications for the M-1 Rail line in Detroit and now runs her own firm, Woods & Watts Effect, as an inclusion, equity, and communications specialist.

Congratulations to 2018 graduates Hannah Blakey (left) and Megan Hutter (right) who received their Certificates of Appointment to the US Military Academy at West Point.

In the class of 2012, three Mercy seniors were named National Merit Finalists. Pictured are Colette Berg (left), Elaina Weber, and Elizabeth Eagle (right).

The hallways of Mercy High can provide spots for quiet discussions. In the above photograph, seniors Gillian Grubb (left) and Elly Bryant catch up by a sunny window in March 2020 near the statue of the Venerable Catherine McAuley, who founded the Sisters of Mercy in 1831 to educate poor girls in Dublin, Ireland. Below, Mercy girls gather in the school's Media Room (previously known as the library) to do homework, check out materials, and be with friends. From left to right around the table are class of 2022 members Samantha Nemer, Maria Norvell, and Isabella Ford, with Sawyer Evans seated on the floor. (Both, photograph by Diane Weiss.)

There are spirited dashes through the hallway on any school day. At left, smiling and reconnecting between classes are Rhys Coleman (left), Nora Dillon (center), and Sawyer Evans, from the class of 2022. Below, raising their voices in song at the Heart of Mercy Mass in March 2020 are, from right to left, Isabella Dimitroff ('23), Valentina Hutter ('23), and Veronica Jude ('22). (Both, photograph by Diane Weiss.)

Mercy's curriculum offers a comprehensive program in liberal arts and sciences while integrating interests outside the classroom. The school also offers Advanced Placement and honors classes in all academic areas, and most recently added AP Computer Science. On average, 80 percent of Mercy students score a three or better on AP exams. Above, biology teacher Lisa Wilson (center) assists students Ava Truman ('20; left) and Katie Kim ('21). Below, in another science class, students Hannah Thomas ('19; left), and Kennedy Eberhart ('20) conduct an experiment.

Every spring, the Heart of Mercy awards are presented to a Mercy senior and teacher nominated by students and staff. The awards, presented after a school-wide Mass, recognize the recipients for exemplifying Mercy's five core values: human dignity, service to others, a commitment to justice, showing mercy, and providing options for the poor. Pictured above in March 2020 are that year's Heart of Mercy recipients—religion teacher Sandra Mals (left) and student Lauren Piziali. Below is Ashley Chichila (right), who, as a Eucharistic minister, is distributing Communion to Brenna VanDenBerg ('22) during the Heart of Mercy Mass. (Both, photograph by Diane Weiss.)

Patricia Sattler is the seventh woman and second layperson to serve as Mercy High principal. She is pictured standing in the entrance that features images and memorabilia from Mercy's 76 years of existence. Sattler previously served as the dean of students at Riverview's Gabriel Richard High School and succeeded Carolyn Witte in 2017. There are no longer Sisters of Mercy available to teach at Mercy High because of the diminished number of women entering religious congregations. (Photograph by Diane Weiss.)

In the 2020–2021 school year, Traci Smith became Mercy's first director of diversity, equity, and inclusion. The position is designed to help the school strive toward a "More Just Mercy" for Mercy's students of color. The murder of George Floyd on May 25, 2020, by a Minneapolis police officer spurred a national outcry, and past and present Mercy students called for change to better address instances of racism. "I am so honored to work at Mercy," Smith said, "to create an anti-racist and anti-biased learning environment."

The rituals of senior year at Mercy High are treasured. In the fall of their senior year, Mercy girls receive their maroon caps and gowns. Pictured below are, from left to right, class of 2019 members Allison Ansara, Aja Underwood, Hannah Thomas, Hallie Buckner, and Sofia Bellisario. Several days before the spring graduation ceremony, Mercy seniors wear their graduation gowns for the Baccalaureate Mass. Above, Mercy president Dr. Cheryl Delaney Kreger hugs a student at the awards ceremony after the Mass.

You cannot have a graduation without a diploma, as shown below. And at Mercy, you cannot have a graduation without dozens of roses, because each young woman must carry a bouquet of them in her arms, as Mercy graduates have done since the school's first graduation ceremony in 1946.

Over the years, the venue for the graduation ceremony has changed. It's no longer held in the school auditorium or on school grounds. For several years, it was held in a reconfigured hockey rink in Plymouth and Meadow Brook Theatre at Oakland University. Since 2013, the ceremony has taken place at the Michigan Opera Theatre in downtown Detroit, a gilded setting for a magnificent ceremony, as illustrated in these photographs.

Pictured onstage at the 2019 Mercy graduation are, from left to right, (first row) Sophie VanderWeele (class salutatorian), Maggie Dwyer, and Jacqueline Hijaouy; (second row) media center staffer Missy Kreucher, fine arts teacher Susan Smith, media center librarian Cheryl Corte, and French teacher Joyce Campbell.

Shayna Jankowski was next in line to receive her diploma and hear her name broadcast throughout the Michigan Opera Theatre during the graduation ceremony in 2018, when associate principal Colleen McMaster called out the names of the graduates.

Members of the Mercyaires chorale group perform at the 2019 graduation. They are, from left to right, Cayla Stus, Kristina Porcalla, Madeleine Surowiec, Kylie Kreucher, Nada Cheaitli, Alaina Beshi, Ainsley Ramirez, Vanessa Aldstadt, Anna Sauer, Tia Hockenhull, Nathalie Gijsbers, Grace Velthoven, Sophia Lyons, and Elise Sikora.

The global COVID-19 pandemic upended life for Mercy and students across the country. In mid-March 2020, Michigan schools were ordered to close. Teachers and students assembled via Zoom or Google Hangout to conduct classes virtually for the remainder of the semester. Above, English and yearbook teacher Hallie Smith meets with the yearbook staff for an update. (Photograph by Harry Smith.)

To mark what would have been their last class day at Mercy, seniors held a drive-through parade in the school parking lot on May 13, 2020. At right, Zhane Coleman is emerging from a vehicle's sunroof to cheer the day. Because of the COVID-19 pandemic shutdown, the class of 2020 missed out on many typical school traditions. "It's really hard because all of it turned around so fast," Macey Earle, student council president, said of the shutdown. "We didn't know that would be the last time we'd . . . walk in the hallways as students."

Mercy cancelled its June 2020 graduation ceremony at the Detroit Opera House. Instead, graduates gathered—masked and six feet apart from each other—in the Detroit Catholic Central High School gym in Novi for the ceremony. Family members could watch via a livestream telecast. Students could elect to wear their maroon robes instead of the traditional white gown. The 185 students in the class of 2020, Mercy's 75th graduating class, were awarded $16 million in college scholarships. Altogether, they served more than 16,000 hours of community service. Among this class were awardees in the National Merit Scholarship Program, including one finalist, two commended seniors, and one Hispanic Scholar. In addition, 19 Mercy graduates earned athletic scholarships. Pictured here are class of 2020 graduates Camille Compton (left), Simone Cotton (center), and Lucy Crampton.

Masks were a required part of the uniform when Mercy High reopened for in-person learning in August 2020. They were a thumbs-up accessory, as indicated by seniors Mya Williams (left), Alexis Butler (center), and Olivia Palm. For the 2020–2021 school year, Mercy utilized both in-person and virtual learning. This hybrid model kept class sizes small and socially-distanced to minimize transmission of COVID-19. Half the student body attended school in person for two days per week, while the other half checked in via computer from home. All school activities were conducted virtually each Wednesday so the school could be thoroughly disinfected.

Christopher Janusch, a computer science and math teacher, was Mercy's 2021 Teacher of the Year. Janusch, pictured here at the 2021 graduation ceremony, also was awarded the Archdiocese of Detroit's 2021 Excellence in Teaching honor. One student commented that he is "an advocate for justice and equality in the classroom and computer science field. His dedication to empowering and teaching girls about tech in a male-dominated field comes from his genuine love for the material."

The Mercy High Class of 2021 received diplomas against the backdrop of the Detroit River. Mercy High's 76th graduation ceremony (above) took place at the Aretha Franklin Amphitheatre in Detroit on June 7, 2021. The open-air venue allowed graduates and their guests to safely participate together, which was more important than ever due to the restrictions necessitated by the COVID-19 pandemic. The class of 2021 numbered 165 graduates, and together they earned more than $12 million in scholarship awards and contributed 11,000 hours of community service. Besides their diplomas and the traditional bouquet of red roses, graduates also received memorial Mercy High laundry bags. Pictured below are, from left to right, Alexandra Beverly, Anna Jain, Sarah Ellsworth, Olivia Haass, Marium Asghar, and Renee Dolenga.

This is where the Mercy girls of today enter an accepting community of learning and challenge in Farmington Hills, Michigan. The symbols on the Mercy school crest, featured at the entrance, illustrate the school's mission. The book symbolizes it as a place of education where moral courage (*virtus*) and knowledge (*scientia*) are fostered under the guidance and protection of Mary, Our Lady of Mercy. The lilies represent a coat for Mary, the Mother of Jesus. Below, spirited graduates take part in one more Mercy tradition—leaping into the future and embodying the school's motto: "Women Who Make a Difference."

About Mercy High School

Mercy High School, the largest all-girls Catholic high school in Michigan, educates young women from Detroit and more than 60 surrounding communities. The school's students mirror the diversity of Detroit with young women who come from multiple cultural, ethnic, faith, and socioeconomic backgrounds. The school's mission statement reads: "Mercy High School, a Catholic college preparatory school immersed in the tradition of the Sisters of Mercy, educates and inspires young women of diverse backgrounds to lead and serve with compassion."

Some basics about Mercy: Among its 90-member staff, 75 percent of them hold master's degrees or higher. Some 20 Mercy alumnae teach or work at the school. Collectively, Mercy teachers have an average of 16 years of teaching experience. Mercy's student–teacher ratio is about 25:1. In the 2020–2021 school year, 655 students were enrolled.

Mercy is one of 42 high schools across America sponsored by the Religious Sisters of Mercy, a religious order with roots in Ireland. The Sisters of Mercy promote values to enhance human dignity, mercy, justice, service, and aid for the poor.

Mercy High tuition for the 2021–2022 school year is $14,550. Mercy awards about $500,000 in financial aid each year.

The class of 2021 earned more than $12 million in scholarship awards and performed more than 11,000 hours of volunteer community service.

Mercy students may take up to seven classes per semester. The school offers a dozen Advanced Placement classes. As a Catholic school, Mercy requires students to take classes in religious studies. The school places an emphasis on morality, theology, and scripture. The school's Campus Ministry Department offers retreats, prayer services, and service projects for students to further explore spiritual formation.

From 2017 through 2019, Mercy High associate principal Larry Baker produced the *Accent on Mercy Alumnae* podcast. It featured dozens of interviews with Mercy alumnae who graduated from 1949 through 2012. Those interviews can be found on Apple Podcasts. The school is on Twitter and Instagram at @MercyHighMI. Mercy High School and the Mercy High School Alumnae Association both have Facebook pages.

To donate to Mercy High, visit www.mhsmi.org/donate or send donations to Mercy High School Advancement Office, 29300 West Eleven Mile Road, Farmington Hills, MI, 48336.

To learn more about Mercy High, visit the school's website at www.mhsmi.org. To learn more about the Sisters of Mercy, visit www.sistersofmercy.org. To learn more about the Mercy Education System of the Americas, visit www.mercyedu.org.